Towards a Global Femicide Index

T0373691

Increasingly there is global attention on the prevalence of women's deaths resulting from intimate partner violence. Campaigns such as 'Counting Dead Women' in Australia, the 'Femicide Census' in England, and the Canadian Femicide Observatory, and the emergence of family violence death review teams globally, build on the work of agencies such as the United Nations and the World Health Organisation, highlighting the fatal consequences of intimate partner violence for women around the world.

This book considers the need for and the steps to be taken towards creating a meaningful framework for a global index of women's deaths from intimate partner violence. While there are global indices for deaths that relate to public violence, such as terrorism, there is to date no systematic global count of killings of women by their intimate partners. It considers the possibilities and challenges that arise in counting intimate femicide. It argues that such an exercise needs to avoid narrow empiricism and instead be part of a broader feminist political project aimed at ending violence against women.

This work will be of great interest to students and scholars of criminology, sociology, law, policing, and politics.

Professor Sandra Walklate is Eleanor Rathbone Chair of Sociology at the University of Liverpool (UK), Professor of Criminology at Monash University (Australia), and Adjunct Professor at QUT (Brisbane, Australia). Internationally recognized for her work in victimology and research on criminal victimization, her recent publications include *A Criminology of War?* (2019, with R. McGarry); *Crime and Emotions: Towards a Criminology of Emotions* (2019, edited collection with M. Hviid-Jacobsen); and *Intimate Partner Violence, Risk and Security* (2018, edited with Kate Fitz-Gibbon, Jude McCulloch, and JaneMaree Maher). She is currently Editor-in-Chief of the *British*

Journal of Criminology, and in 2014 she was given the British Society of Criminology's outstanding achievement award.

Dr Kate Fitz-Gibbon is Senior Lecturer in Criminology in the School of Social Sciences at Monash University (Australia) and Lead Researcher in the Monash Gender and Family Violence Prevention Centre. Her research examines family violence, the law of homicide, and the impact of criminal law reform across Australian and international jurisdictions. This research has been undertaken with a focus on gender, responsibility, and justice. Dr Fitz-Gibbon has advised on homicide law and family violence reform in several Australian and international jurisdictions. Recent publications include *Intimate Partner Violence, Risk and Security* (2018, edited with Sandra Walklate, Jude McCulloch, and JaneMaree Maher); *Homicide, Gender and Responsibility: An International Perspective* (2016, edited with Sandra Walklate); *Homicide Law Reform in Victoria: Retrospect and Prospects* (2015, edited with Arie Freiberg); and *Homicide Law Reform, Gender and the Provocation Defence* (2014).

Professor Jude McCulloch is Professor of Criminology at Monash University (Australia) and the inaugural Director of the Monash Gender and Family Violence Prevention Centre. She leads a diverse research programme on family violence prevention. Prior to her academic career, she worked in a women's refuge and as a community lawyer, providing legal assistance and support to women victims of crime as well as engaging in campaigns around gender and justice. The Australasian Council of Women and Policing awarded her the Griffith University Prize for excellence in research in improving policing for women. Jude is an expert on risk, security, policing, and terrorism. Her current research compares responses to the risk of family violence and terrorism and the impacts of these different approaches on women's security.

Professor JaneMaree Maher is Professor and Director of the Centre for Women's Studies and Gender Research Sociology at Monash University. She works on gendered violence and hate crimes using feminist legal paradigms. Her research more broadly addresses family and gender issues, with a focus on women's caring and employment in family life. Recent book publications include *Policing Hate Crime: Understanding Communities and Prejudice* (2017, with G. Mason, J. Maher, J. McCulloch, S. Pickering, R. Wickes, and C. McKay) and *Sex Work: Labour, Mobility and Sexual Services* (2013, with S. Pickering and A. Gerard).

Towards a Global Femicide Index

Counting the Costs

**Sandra Walklate,
Kate Fitz-Gibbon, Jude McCulloch,
and JaneMaree Maher**

LONDON AND NEW YORK

First published 2020 by Routledge

2 Park Square, Milton Park, Abingdon, Oxon OX14 4RN

605 Third Avenue, New York, NY 10017

Routledge is an imprint of the Taylor & Francis Group, an informa business

First issued in paperback 2021

Publisher's Note

The publisher has gone to great lengths to ensure the quality of this reprint but points out that some imperfections in the original copies may be apparent.

British Library Cataloguing-in-Publication Data
A catalogue record for this book is available from the British Library

Library of Congress Cataloging-in-Publication Data
A catalog record has been requested for this book

ISBN: 978-1-138-38908-3 (hbk)
ISBN: 978-1-03-217607-9 (pbk)
DOI: 10.4324/9781138393134

Typeset in Times New Roman
by codeMantra

This book is dedicated to all those across the world who work tirelessly to prevent violence against women.

Contents

Preface   viii
Acknowledgements   x

Introduction: 'setting the scene'   1

1   How do we count? Mapping global approaches
    to counting women's deaths   19

2   Trends in counting: what do the numbers mean?   33

3   Why counting matters: the opportunities and
    benefits of counting intimate femicide   46

4   The risks of counting the killing of women   60

5   Using data on intimate femicide to inform risk   75

    Conclusion: looking to the future – from
    counting to preventing?   94

Index   105

Preface

Women matter. Killing women matters. Counting the number of women killed is an important part of making it visible. It needs to be made visible to the public, policy makers, and politicians.

The gendering of homicide statistics requires more than identifying the sex of the victim. It needs the sex of the perpetrator. It needs the identification of any gendered relationship between perpetrator and victim. This includes an intimate partnership and other family relationships. It also includes sexuality, as when a killing is part of rape. Potentially it can include a range of gendered motivations, including, for example, deaths linked to dowry and to so-called 'honour'.

The gendering of homicide statistics should be simple and obvious. It should be a routine part of official statistics on crime. But it appears that not all think it is simple and obvious, especially statistical bodies and other public policy entities engaged in the processing of unlawful death.

This excellent book explores the nuances and complexities in the processes of making visible the gendered killing of women. It balances the need to count with awareness of the dangers that incorrect forms of simplification might generate. It argues for a global femicide index while acknowledging the difficulties in implementing the apparently simple statement that the killing of women can be a gendered killing of women.

The book promotes the improvement in the collection of data on the gendered killing of women within a wider framework concerning the policies and politics required to reduce gender-based violence.

In order to improve statistics on the gender of killing, it is necessary to engage with debates on the contested conceptualization of gender. This engagement is a strength of the book.

Feminism and counting are not incompatible projects. The book endorses the need of the feminist project to become more involved in improving statistics, rather than rejecting statistics. It should not be surprising to write this.

Counting femicide requires difficult engagement with theories of gender and theories of violence. This is the strength of this project and why it is successful in destabilizing orthodoxies.

Sylvia Walby O.B.E.
Professor of Sociology and Director of the
Violence and Society Centre
City University, U.K.

Acknowledgements

This book is part of a wider project and team work emanating from the Gender and Family Violence Prevention Centre at Monash University (Australia). The authors owe a debt of gratitude to the rest of the team working with us at the centre. In particular we are grateful for the support of Dr Jasmine McGowan and Kate Thomas (now working for Australia's National Research Organisation for Women's Safety) for keeping the work of the centre going whilst we were writing this book. We would also like to acknowledge the important contribution of Dr Rachel Burgin, who compiled a literature review for us in preparation for this project. Thanks also to Professor Sylvia Walby, who gave her time to write a preface for this book.

Throughout this project, we have benefited from the insights and expertise of many feminist scholars. We would like to thank those who attended the Intimate partner violence, risk and security workshop at Monash Prato in September 2017, which resulted in the edited collection, Fitz-Gibbon, K., Walklate, S., McCulloch, J. & Maher, J. (eds) (2018) Intimate Partner Violence, Risk and Security: Securing Women's Lives in a Global World (London: Routledge). We would also like to thank all those who attended the workshop held at the University of Liverpool in London in June 2019, funded by the School of Law and Social Justice at Liverpool University, where some of the ideas presented here were subjected to closer critical scrutiny. The inspirational contributions at that workshop made by Professor Nadera Shalhoub-Kevorkian and Professor Sylvia Walby sharpened our thinking in many ways, as did the comments of all those who attended a national roundtable on femicide data collection in August 2019 organized by the Monash Centre. The roundtable brought together experts, practitioners, and academics from around Australia, including judicial officers, death review personnel, journalists, Australia's National Research Organisation for Women's Safety, a Churchill Fellow researching death review processes internationally, and academics researching intimate femicide and violence against women. Thanks are also due to those who listened to a presentation of this work at the 3rd European Conference on Domestic Violence held in Oslo in September 2019.

This book is an outcome from the Australian Research Council– funded project Securing women's lives: Preventing intimate partner homicide, led by Professor Jude McCulloch with Dr Kate Fitz-Gibbon, Professor JaneMaree Maher, and Professor Sandra Walklate (DP170100706).

Introduction
'Setting the scene'

Introduction

It is estimated that on average 137 women across the world are killed by an intimate partner or a family member every day (UNODC 2018). Over a 12-month period, this equates to the killing of 50,005 women worldwide. In El Salvador, the country with the highest femicide rate in Latin America, this translates to the killing of a woman every 18 hours (Donovan 2019). In Asia, 20,000 women in 2017 alone were killed by their intimate partner or family members. In Australia, where family violence has been declared a national emergency, at least one woman every week is killed by an intimate partner or a family member. In Mexico, seven women are killed each day (Madrigal 2017). When we focus specifically on the killing of women by their male intimate partners, the statistics remain just as confronting. In England and Wales, it is estimated that at least two women are killed each week by a current or former intimate partner (Office for National Statistics 2016), while in Canada, it is estimated that a woman or girl is killed every 2.5 days (Canadian Femicide Observatory for Justice and Accountability 2019). The number of women killed is now recognized as being of such gravity that in numerous countries worldwide violence against women has been labelled a national crisis. The counting of women's deaths has been one key strategy in ensuring that these individual lives are accounted for and that collectively these deaths are understood as a critical constituent of the costs of global violence against women.

This increased attention to violence against women globally has meant that action against femicide is progressing on the agendas of national governments and regional and international bodies. Consistent with this in 2016, under the leadership of the Special Rapporteur on violence against women, the United Nations (UN) called for the establishment of femicide watches or observatories in every country, arguing that

> [u]nless there is accurate and comparable data collection on a given crime, there will be no proper understanding of it and no effective strategy with which to combat it. Having clear data helps law makers and government officials win the public's support for tackling it through targeted prevention and investigation resources. Femicide has been defined as murder of a woman by an intimate partner or family members and the targeting of women by criminal gangs or as a weapon of war. It has been universally recognised as a crime. But how do horrific crimes of this type so often slip under the radar? Why is it so difficult to collect data on such an abhorrent criminal activity and, subsequently, to arrest the perpetrators?
>
> (ACUNS 2017: 1)

This book critically examines the possibilities and problems that might arise in light of this call. Specifically, it reflects on how we understand the relationship between counting such killings and preventing them: how might the collection of country-specific data towards a global femicide index advance and/or hinder efforts to prevent femicides? We focus specifically on the killing of women by their male intimate partners/ex-partners as the most common form of femicide. Worldwide, intimate partner violence – that is, abusive behaviour by a person within an intimate relationship, including current or past marriages, domestic partnerships, de facto or dating relationships – is the most prevalent form of violence against women (see, for example, World Health Organisation 2010). Intimate partner homicide is the most extreme expression of intimate partner violence (World Health Organisation 2012, 2013). Yet there is a dearth of dependable and comprehensive data about these killings at the national level in most countries and jurisdictions. As a result, there is no reliable global tally of such deaths.

The rationale for more systematic collection of femicide data is to better prevent such killings, though it is recognized that pathways to prevention are long, complex, and difficult to map or track with any accuracy. The term 'data' is a broad one, which in this context embraces a range of different ways of knowing, including the call for observatories and watches. References to accuracy and comparability of data, alongside the UN's focus on measuring and counting, suggest that the call for more data on femicide is primarily a call for greater attention to counting, to better quantitative information on how many women are killed by their (ex)-partners. Measuring or counting violence against women broadly, and intimate partner homicide in particular, will not independently prevent or reduce such violence or address the high level of impunity often attached to these crimes. We argue, however, that the more systematic collection of national data on the number of femicides as part of work towards the establishment of a global femicide index should not be just a technical exercise. It could instead be conceived as the product of political action to make such crimes more visible, as a way of better understanding the prevalence, nature, and circumstances of such killings, and to commit to the type of changes (social, legal, cultural, economic, and political) necessary to ultimately prevent these deaths and end these crimes (see Vives-Cases et al. 2016, on technical steps and political action in data collection on femicide). Such a political project could both reflect and be a platform for a diversity of actions and aspirations contributing to ending violence against women. Counting and measuring femicide and critiquing counting and measuring femicide might then be conceived as dual strategies in a broader political project aimed at revealing the full extent of such violence as well as ending violence against women.

Why counting matters

Marilyn Waring, in her foundational contribution to feminist economics *If Women Counted* (1988) later published as *Counting for Nothing: What Men Value and Women Are Worth* (1999), is instructive on this topic. Her original influential book revealed the invisibility of women's domestic labour and how this invisibility was institutionalized in the systems of national accounts. Waring highlights the failure to recognize women's work outside the formal labour force and the many policy implications for women of not being counted as workers contributing to national wealth. The first edition of her book focused on the failure to count women's domestic labour and ways to better account for it. In the book's second edition, published 11 years later, Waring reflects on counting as a tool and the tensions, implicit but unarticulated, in the first edition. Here she reflects on her deeper understanding and later recognition that counting alone would not be enough to rectify the injustice flowing from the failure to fully recognize women's labour. She asks herself to what extent could making women's domestic labour visible through national accounts be effective in capturing the real value of women's labour and positively impact policy, and 'at what point would patriarchy reassert its power'? (Waring 1999: 10). In the decade or so between publication of the first and second editions of her book, bodies such as the UN and the International Labor Organisation (ILO) appeared to have taken into account feminist's arguments by imputing a value to women's domestic labour. Waring, however, reflects that in using economic models, particularly quantification and accounting as a strategy or a tool against the invisibility of women's domestic labour, she had

> underestimated the willingness of the ideologues and the practitioners to construct even more abstractions, regardless of the model's relationship to human experience. I underestimated the capacity for unreality.
>
> (1999: xxi)

Essentially, Waring points out that without changing the foundation of the economic system, which fails to value women's labour, and the broader system, patriarchy, which fails to value women, being counted is not necessarily a victory. She states that in pressing for the counting of women's domestic labour in her first book, her 'short-term policy needs for visibility were at odds with my passionate desire to bring this system to its knees' (1999: xx–xxi). Waring's reflection highlights that in seeking transformative social change, as feminist projects tend to, there will be few decisive victories. Instead, it is necessary to consider tools that can be used strategically, tested, reflected upon, adjusted, or abandoned as circumstances change and lessons are learned. It is also necessary to acknowledge that many of the tools used will be compromised and compromising, as a result of being generated and embedded in ways of knowing which have historically been blind to, and/or profoundly unsympathetic to, women's lived experience. As Elizabeth Grosz (1986) contended, diverse feminist interventions will have to be applied tactically and dynamically in order to achieve change.

This book is written in the spirit of feminist political action. As such it is not primarily focused on the technical steps required to establish and maintain femicide watches or observatories. Nor is it concerned with spelling out how we would gather these figures together towards achieving a global count or femicide index. Instead, we consider what might be gained or learned, and what might be lost or hidden, in the process of global attempts to count femicide systematically. The book critically engages with the assumptions and epistemologies that underpin calls for counting, along with the counting itself. It seeks to harness some of the lessons of history, particularly the lessons of other feminist and social justice projects, in considering what place counting and measuring might have in working towards the goal of ending violence against women, especially the lethal violence inflicted by men on their female intimate partners. We ask how counting femicide might be used as a political strategy to advance the goal of ending violence against women and equally what the risks are of femicide counts being co-opted into the knowledges of a world order that generates and perpetuates violence against women in all its forms.

Counting matters in the global context

The UN Sustainable Development Agenda (SDA) 2030, adopted in 2015, includes the goal of eliminating all forms of violence against all women and girls (Target 5.2). The Under-Secretary-General and Executive Director of UN Women said at the time of the adoption of this agenda: 'Data on their own will not change lives, but we will not change lives without them' (quoted UN 2016: 16). The change sought, through the more comprehensive and effective counting of femicides, is ultimately the prevention of gendered killings. However, setting an agenda to prevent violence against women of all types is complex, multilayered, and multifaceted (Heise 2011). More than 35 years ago, Elizabeth Wilson, in a book entitled *What Is to Be Done about Violence against Women?* published in 1983, maintained that any agenda for change required action at the level of social policy, law, and ideology. Counting intimate femicides could be part of an approach that addresses each of these different levels. Alternatively, counting might in myriad ways reproduce the types of power dynamics and gendered assumptions that give rise to male violence against women, including lethal violence. Femicide counts may obscure the gendered patterns underpinning such violence: individual incidents and events might stand in for recognition of the social and political structures, thereby facilitating and enabling gendered violence. However, as individual events they do not necessarily render those structures visible. They are locked in a moment in time, and of course structures reveal themselves over time. As the quote from Marilyn Waring above suggests, while numbers are powerfully associated with objectivity, they may produce 'evidence' that bears little resemblance to reality, particularly when that reality is women's lived experiences of violence, inequality, and marginalization.

Walby and Towers (2017) argue that in order to prevent violence against women in all its forms, we need to be able to test various theories about what causes violence through the effective measurement of such violence. What needs to be kept in mind, however, is counting, while not a theory, is a way of knowing that itself needs to be, if not tested, then carefully interrogated in terms of its ability to add value to what is known about violence against women over and through time. It is unlikely that counting or measuring will add to what we need to know in order to effectively prevent lethal violence against women, unless such counts are produced as part of a broader political commitment that fully acknowledges gendered power relations as they intersect with other hierarchical power relations related to ongoing colonial relations of power (Dala and Robertson 2004), ableism (Madriaga and Mallett 2010), class, and heteronormativity.

A reflection on sources and types of data on violence against women, the utility of different types of data, and how it is being interpreted is timely, if not overdue. Many governments worldwide alongside the UN are presently engaging in substantive reviews of responses to intimate partner violence, intimate partner homicides, and femicide (see, for example, UN 2016). In 2013, the issue reached the pinnacle of the international political agenda when the United Nations Commission on Crime Prevention and Criminal Justice's resolution on the gender-related killing of women was adopted by the General Assembly (UN 2016: 12). As part of this the UN has encouraged Member States 'to collect, disaggregate, analyse and report data on the gender-related killing of women and girls' (UN 2016: 22). This directive at the international level assumes a degree of agreement as to what forms of violence are included under the broad banner of 'gender-related killing'. To date, however, definitions of what 'counts' as gender-related killing have been blurred and inconsistent across countries, regions, cultures, and political contexts.

Why definitions matter

Femicide is the gender-based killing of women and the most extreme form of violence against women. Diana Russell used the term 'femicide' at the International Tribunal on Crimes against Women in 1976 to refer to the intentional 'killings of females by males because they are females' (Russell 2001). In Latin America 'femicide' and 'feminicide' are the accepted terms for such crimes (Pierobom de Avila 2018). Femicide occurs in a range of contexts, including intimate partner violence, armed conflict, dowry disputes, sexual violence, and the protection of family 'honour' (UN 2016: 10). A broader definition includes the responsibility of states for femicides (Vives-Cases et al. 2016) through the propagation of discriminatory or exclusionary laws or policies and/or the failure of state agencies to act and to protect. However, the term 'femicide' in itself ensures that the nature, extent, and impact of patriarchal social relations are not lost in the process of defining what is to be counted and why it is to be counted. As both Dekeseredy (2019) and Sheehy (2018) have cogently argued, non-neutral terminology is central to avoiding what Fraser (2009) has called the 'cunning of history' in silencing the feminist concern with oppression (see also Pease 2019). Consequently, definitions matter because they change the numbers of killings that can be counted and therefore impact upon our understandings of patterns of extreme gendered violence. On another level, they matter because they signal to the community what and who 'counts': who is and who is not included in such counts. (For example, the recent response to the work of Walby and Towers (2018) illustrated in the work of Donovan and Barnes (2019) stands as testimony to the ongoing contestation of terms and definitions within this field of inquiry.) Nonetheless, the term 'femicide' itself emerged as a way to register the importance of gender and sex in the patterns of homicide across the globe.

There are various estimates of the number of women killed worldwide every year (see, for example, Secretariat 2011; Small Arms Survey 2016). Although all of these estimates put the number of women killed globally substantially lower than the number of men killed, the killing of women typically occurs in specific contexts where gendered social hierarchies are critical. It is here that women are disproportionately victimized. Stöckl et al. (2013) found in their global study that approximately 14 per cent of all homicides were committed by intimate partners and that 39 per cent of female homicide victims were killed by intimate partners compared to only 6 per cent of all male homicide victims. In high-income countries, they found that 41 per cent of female victims of homicide were killed by an intimate partner (see also UN 2014: 14).

This book focuses on the most common form of femicide, the killing of women by their male intimate partners. As femicide refers to the gender-related killing of women, it could be argued that its categorization relies more so on the motive of the killer than the relationship between the victim and the offender. However, the killing of women by their male partners is typically assumed to be a gendered killing as the relationship, and the power and control dynamics within it, is central to the killing (see, for example, Pierobom de Avila 2018). Intimate partner homicides represent the extreme end of the spectrum of intimate partner violence. Intimate partner homicides are homicides where the victim and offender are current or former intimates, whether married, de facto partners, or boy/girlfriend. As noted earlier, although the specific rates vary by country, as a general pattern, women are vastly over-represented as victims in domestic homicides. Bridger et al. (2017) found in their study of heterosexual intimate partner homicide cases in England and Wales that 86 per cent of perpetrators were male, and 14 per cent female. Australian studies have found that women account for over 75 per cent of intimate partner homicide victims (Cussen and Bryant 2015). Similar gendered patterns are evident in other countries and extend to intimate femicides where the perpetrator goes on to commit suicide. For example, in the United States 94 per cent of all victims of intimate femicide-suicides are female (Violence Policy Center 2012).

Our focus in this book is intimate partner homicides, where the victim is a woman and the perpetrator is a man, that is, the typical gendered scenario of intimate partner violence and intimate partner homicide. Intimate partner homicides of women are sometimes referred to as intimate femicide or intimate partner femicide (World Health Organisation 2012). There is some tension between the terms 'femicide' and 'homicide' in describing intimate killings (Pierobom de Avila 2018). The term 'intimate partner homicide' highlights the context of the killing but not its gendered nature. Femicide highlights the gendered nature of the homicide but does not specifically indicate the context in which femicide most typically occurs. Our decision, throughout this book, is to use the term 'intimate femicide' to refer to intimate partner homicides involving a female victim and a male perpetrator who have or have had an intimate relationship with one another.

Why language matters

In writing this book, we returned often to the issue of language. What terms or phrases best work to capture, acknowledge, recognize, and respect the gravity, sadness, and tragedy of a woman's death at the hands of a male partner? If we use the word 'death', we focus on the loss of a woman's life but do we focus sufficiently on the agent of her death and his responsibility? Further, does the presence of a dead body adequately capture the absence of living a life without the violence, fear, and control that can all too often lead to a woman's early death? (Sherman and Harris 2015). (Whilst this question might raise a bigger issue in relation to what is understood by violence, it also serves to remind us, following Waring, that being counted and counting as a valued life are not necessarily the same thing.) Moreover, is 'men's lethal violence against women' a good way of capturing the violent nature of the death and making the perpetrator fully visible in the frame? Is the word 'killing' more appropriate than 'death' when referring to a femicide because it highlights responsibility and removes any suggestion that the death was accidental, natural, or timely? We concluded that no term or phrase was adequate. Perhaps the inadequacy of language is why the intervention of feminist artists is powerful in memorializing the lethal violence inflicted upon women by men (see, for example, Lozier 2018). Art and performance in various mediums seem well suited to evoking the impact of violent death through the symbolic presence of absent women: whether red shoes in Mexico standing in memoriam for femicide victims (Telesur 2016) or red dresses in Canada blowing in the wind reminding us of First Nations women killed (Coorsh 2015). Though inadequate, throughout this book, we have endeavoured to use language that honours the women taken by intimate femicide, emphasizes that their deaths were violent, and points to men as the perpetrators of that violence.

Femicide matters globally

Research consistently shows that intimate partner violence is a global issue, not exclusive to any one country, culture, or socio-economic group. It is, however, a gendered form of violence. The drivers of gender violence, and intimate partner violence, as the most common type of such violence, are consistently linked to gender inequality. This inequality is manifest in many subtle, obvious, and diverse ways across the globe: from the wages gap, the absence or limited presence of women in leadership positions in politics and in public space, the exclusion of women from education, to the refusal to ensure women's educational achievements translate into careers that match those of their less educated male counterparts, to mention but a few examples. One study across 44 countries found that factors relating to gender inequality predicted the level of prevalence of intimate partner violence (Heise and Kotsadam 2015). Intimate femicide, as the most extreme form of intimate partner violence, is then linked to gender inequality (see, for example, United Nations 2011).

Lack of data and differences in the way, and extent to which, different countries currently count intimate femicide makes prevalence comparisons across nations and across time difficult. Despite issues with incomplete data, available evidence suggests the number of intimate femicides has not decreased but rather remained stable or increased in recent decades (Brennan 2016 in the United Kingdom; Cussen and Bryant 2015 in Australia; Smith et al. 2014 in the United States;

UNODC 2018). Researchers have noted, for example, that '[t]he decline in overall homicide in England and Wales over the past decade has not been matched by declines in intimate partner homicide (IPH), which now make up one in five of all homicides' (Bridger et al. 2017: 94) though there is some debate concerning the most recent figures with ONS (2018) reporting that during 2017 the least number of women were killed by their partner/ex-partner in the last 40 years. Even where intimate homicides are decreasing, the decrease appears to be linked to a drop in the number of male victims (see Dawson et al. 2009; Fox and Zawitz 2004) rather than to a reduction in intimate femicide per se. The continuing prevalence of intimate femicide is often linked to the persistence of discriminatory social structures and gender inequality, as a primary driver of violence against women. Yet, even in countries that enjoy high levels of gender equality such as Sweden, gendered violence and intimate femicide persist (Fundamental Rights Agency 2014). The intractability of intimate femicide, despite an increasing focus on violence against women and gender inequality in many jurisdictions and globally, has underpinned calls to continue to build an evidence base about the number and nature of these killings.

The data on the nature and prevalence of femicide, particularly intimate femicide, is increasing worldwide (World Health Organisation 2012). Until relatively recently, intimate femicide tended not to be counted as a separate homicide category in most national databases. Increasingly, however, we count and recognize the costs of violence against women, including by counting the number of women killed by men. Campaigns by feminist civil society groups such as 'Counting Dead Women' in Australia (Cullen et al. 2018; Destroy the Joint 2018), the 'Femicide Census' in England (Brennan 2016), and the Canadian Femicide Observatory (Dawson 2018), combined with more institutionalized exercises such as family violence death reviews (see, for example Dawson 2017), represent significant if nascent steps towards more systematic counting of intimate femicides. To date, however, there are still only a small number of countries that have specific registries of intimate femicides (Vives-Cases et al. 2016).

The failure to systematically count intimate femicides can be seen as a reflection on the lack of value accorded to women's lives. Not being counted, in death as in life, can be read as a sign of not being seen to count (Porter 1996). While intimate femicide is increasingly recognized as a serious legal, human rights, and public health issue of global dimensions, the risk of such violence is not taken as seriously as other forms of violence, like, for example, deaths from terrorist activity (Fitz-Gibbon et al. 2018: 5–7). Since the September 11, 2001 attacks on the United States, deaths from terrorist activity have been accorded the status of being the West's number one security issue (Buzan and Wæver 2009; Ericson 2006). Yet, as we have argued elsewhere, intimate femicide represents a far greater threat to life, particularly in Western countries (Walklate et al. 2019). Since 2012, consistent with the priority given to terrorism as a global security issue, there has been a global terrorism index to 'measure and understand terrorism'. The most recent figures indicate there were 25,673 deaths from terrorist attacks in 2016. This was a decrease of 13 per cent from 2015 (Institute of Economics and Peace 2017: 4). In comparison, according to the most recent report of United Nations Office on Drugs and Crime (UNODC) on the gender-related killing of women and girls, 87,000 women were victims of homicide in 2017, of which 50,000 'were killed by intimate partners or family members', while 30,000 of those women were 'killed by their current or former intimate partner'. This was an increase from an estimated 48,000 killings of women by an intimate partner or family member in 2012 (UNODC 2018: 10). Perhaps in this respect the counts 'speak' for themselves.

The costs of counting and not counting

To be explicit the costs that are the focus of this book are not 'simply' economic, though the import and significance of the economic costs of gendered violence(s) to global, regional, and national economies should not be under-estimated. Walby and Olive (2014), for example, estimate that gender-based violence costs the European economy over 109 billion euros a year with the Assistant Secretary-General and Deputy Executive Director of UN Women Lakshmi Puri (September 21st 2018) stating: 'research indicates that the cost of violence against women could amount to around 2 per cent of the global gross domestic product (GDP). This is equivalent to $1.5 trillion'. The economic costs of femicide are a constituent element of these global figures. This is especially the case if we configure our understanding of femicide as the culmination of the slow violence(s) figures such as these reflect.

Nixon (2011: 2) defines slow violence as

> a violence of delayed destruction that is dispersed across time and space, an attritional violence that is typically not viewed as violence at all.

Following Nixon (2011) and Wonders' (2018) more recent extension of this into slow intimate partner violence, here our vision of counting embraces an appreciation of the costs of gender-based violence as they are intimately connected with, and articulated through, what might be called slow femicide. The economic, physical, mental, and social costs – some of which are counted in the figures cited above; in addition, some of these costs are less tangible like anxiety, sleep loss, and so on (see Matos and Goncalves 2019) – constitute quality of life costs to women. These might be expressed as the living death of slow femicide, which rather like the family secrets explored by Barnwell (2019) can reach down through the generations. So the costs of counting the violent incident-related deaths of femicide are that we run the risk of denying the living death of slow femicide and the temporal connections between femicide and slow femicide. Making these links explicit serves to remind us that femicide is more often than not, though not always, the culmination of a process rather than a stand-alone incident. Thus any count is only ever a partial recognition of the slow femicide of many women's lives. This can be seen as one of the costs of quantification. Moreover, there are further costs inherent in the act of counting requiring explication.

In exploring the call for the more systematic collection of data on femicide and intimate femicide in particular, this book unpacks the implications of data collection patterns and practices in terms of local, regional, national, and global policy responses and feminist projects of preventing and accounting for the killings of women by male intimate partners. We focus on the counting work that exists, its rationale, and how this might be strengthened and extended. Our discussion recognizes the myriad risks of counting as a technical process if it disconnected from a broader feminist project linked to addressing the drivers of such violence. Such a project encompasses ending violence against women in all its forms and valuing the lives of 'everybody', including women, especially First Nations women and women of colour, whose deaths are disproportionate in number and often rendered invisible or disappeared. Femicide has been characterized as 'often the final and most serious consequence of pervasive discrimination, including acts of violence' (UN 2016: 10–11). The intersecting structural discrimination attached to gendered and colonial relations of power renders First Nations women and women of colour particularly vulnerable to violence and violent death, with similar intersecting discrimination and danger impacting on women with disability (Maher et al. 2018).

The field of homicide studies is replete with books aiming to introduce the reader to the general features and responses to homicide as a specific crime. With the exception of the groundbreaking edited collection by Radford and Russell (1992) *Femicide: the politics of woman killing* and the body of work by Dobash and Dobash (2015), little attention has been paid to the specific characteristics of intimate femicide. Recently more focused scholarly attention has been given to the role of monitoring and policy reviews as a means of addressing the nature and extent of intimate partner homicide (Dawson 2017). However, with the exception of Merry (2016) and the programme of work led by Walby and others (2017), little detailed attention has been given to the problems of measurement in relation to violence against women generally and femicide in particular. We agree with Merry that we need not be seduced by the powers of quantification, but we do need to consider what can be achieved by counting, for whom, in what context, and how such counting practices facilitate or fail to facilitate any preventive agenda. This book is the first to reflect on the problems, possibilities, and costs of counting, or failing to count, intimate femicide.

Outline of this book

We aim to set out the different ways in which intimate femicide is presently counted and accounted for. This book is intended to inform students, policy makers, academics, journalists, and feminist activists about intimate femicides and what might be achieved by better counting this form of gendered killing. It also carefully considers the limits and potential dangers of quantification as a way of understanding and addressing this phenomenon. It asks critical questions about how we move from better quantification towards transformative approaches to prevention. Our objective is to provide a gendered background for the pattern and prevalence of these killings, which is simultaneously attentive to geographical and cultural specificities. This gendered foundation is central in order to develop a critical framework to inform future policies, practices, and processes that will ensure these killings count and are accounted for in ways consistent with the realities of women's lives.

Chapter 1 looks at how intimate femicides are currently counted, maps global approaches to counting such killings, and discusses the gaps in such counting. Chapter 2 explores what the numbers tell us in terms of women's risk at the country, regional, and global level and whose deaths are invisibilized in this 'counts'. Chapter 3 considers why we should count intimate femicide, critically analysing the benefits likely to arise from national registers and a global index. In Chapter 4, we consider the risks of counting women's deaths, including the foundation of counting practice and what this means for the counts that emerge, the challenges of retaining the meaning of each individual life when counting the collective, as well as the question of 'who' counts, 'what' counts, and how these may serve to render invisible particular patterns of violence (for example, in diverse communities) and particular patterns of violence (for example, murder suicides). Chapter 5 examines the intersections between counting intimate femicide and understanding, assessing, and managing risk of serious harm and death. The concluding chapter looks to counting and the future of a global intimate femicide index as one possible strategy or tool in the transformative feminist project of preventing and eliminating violence against women.

References

Academic Council on the United Nations System. (2017). *Femicide VII: Establishing a Femicide Watch in Every Country*. Vienna: ACUNS.

Barnwell, A. (2019). Family secrets and the slow violence of social stigma. *Sociology*. doi:10.1177/0038038519846443

Brennan, D. (2016). *Femicide Census Profiles of Women Killed by Men: Redefining an Isolated Incident*. London: Women's Aid.

Bridger, E., Strang, H., Parkinson, J., and Sherman, L. (2017). Intimate partner homicide in England and Wales 2011–2013: pathways to prediction from multi-agency domestic homicide reviews. *Cambridge Journal of Evidence Based Policing*, 1: 93. doi:10.1007/s41887-017-0013-z

Buzan, B. and Wæver, O. (2009). Macrosecuritisation and security constellations: reconsidering scale in securitisation theory. *View of International Studies*, 35(2): 253–276.

Canadian Femicide Observatory for Justice and Accountability (2019). Centre for the Study of Social and Legal Responses to violence. Available at: https://www.femicideincanada.ca/home/newsroom

Coorsh, K. (2015). Red dresses honour Canada's missing and murdered Aboriginal Women. *CTV News*. October 4 2015. Available at: www.ctvnews.ca/canada/red-dresses-honour-canada-s-missing-murdered-aboriginal-women-1.2594856

Cullen, P., Vaughan, G., Zhuoyang, L., Price, J., Yu, D., and Sullivan, E. (2018). Counting dead women in Australia: an in-depth case review of femicide. *Journal of Family Violence*, 34: 1. doi:10.1007/s10896-018-9963-6

Cussen, T. and Bryant, W. (2015). Domestic/family homicide in Australia, Research in Practice no. 38, Australian Institute of Criminology.

Dalea, R. and Robertson, S. (2004). Interview with Boaventura de Sousa Santos. *Globalisation, Societies and Education*, 2(2): 147–160.

Dawson, M. (Ed). (2017). *Domestic Homicides and Death Reviews: An International Perspective*. London: Palgrave Macmillan.

Dawson, M. (2018). The Canadian femicide observatory for justice and accountability report. Available at: https://femicideincanada.ca

Dawson, M., Bunge, V.P., and Balde, T. (2009). National trends in intimate partner homicides: explaining the decline, Canada 1976–2001. *Violence against Women*, 15: 276–306.

Dekeseredy, W. (2019). Bringing feminist sociological analysis of patriarchy back to the forefront of the study of woman abuse. Paper presented to the 3rd European Conference on Domestic Violence, Oslo, September.

Destroy the Joint. (2018). Counting dead women. Available at: https://www.facebook.com/DestroyTheJoint/

Dobash, R.E. and Dobash, R.P. (2015). *When Men Murder Women*. Oxford: Oxford University Press.

Donovan, L. (2019). 'Men kill women because they can': inside El Salvador's devastating femicide crisis. Elle UK. Available at: www.elle.com/uk/life-and-culture/a25626891/el-salvador-femicide-crisis/

Donovan, C. and Barnes, R. (2019). Re-tangling the concept of coercive control: a view from the margins and a response to Walby and Towers (2018). *Criminology and Criminal Justice*. doi:10.1177/1748895819864622

Ericson, R.V. (2006). Ten uncertainties of risk management approaches to security. *Canadian Journal of Criminology and Criminal Justice*, 48(3): 345–356.

Fitz-Gibbon, K., Walklate, S., McCulloch, J., and Maher, J. (2018). Introduction intimate partner violence, risk and security – securing women's lives in a global world. In K. Fitz-Gibbon, S. Walklate, J. McCulloch, and J.M. Maher (eds) *Intimate Partner Violence, Risk and Security: Securing Women's Lives in a Global World*, pp. 1–16. London: Routledge.

Fox, J.A. and Zawitz, M.W. (2004). Homicide trends in the United States: 2002 update. Crime Brief, Office of Justice Programs, Bureau of Justice Statistics.

Fraser, N. (2009). Feminism, capitalism and the cunning of history. *New Left Review*, 56: 97–117.

Fundamental Rights Agency. (2014). *Violence against Women: An EU-wide Survey*. Vienna: European Union Agency for Fundamental Rights.

Grosz, E. (1986). What is feminist theory. In C. Pateman and E. Grosz (eds) *Feminist Challenges: Social and Political Theory*, pp. 190–204. Sydney: Allen and Unwin.

Heise, L. and Kotsadam, A. (2015). Cross-national and multi-level correlates of partner violence: an analysis of data from population-based surveys. *Lancet Global Health*, 3: 332–340.

Heise, L. (2011). What works to prevent partner violence?: An evidence overview. Working paper. Organisation for Economic Cooperation and Development. Available at: https://www.oecd.org/derec/unitedkingdom/49872444.pdf

Institute of Economics and Peace. (2017). Vision of humanity. Available at: http://visionofhumanity.org/indexes/terrorism-index/

Lozier, L. (2018). Mapping gender violence narratives in the Northern Triangle of Central America. In K. Fitz-Gibbon, S. Walklate, J. McCulloch and J. Maree Maher (eds) *Intimate Partner Violence, Risk and Security: Securing Women's Lives in a Global World* (pp. 109–125).London and New York: Routledge.

Madrigal, S. (2017). La Muerte Sale por el Oriente: a collaborative artistic project about femicide in Mexico. In H. Hemblade, A. Filip, A. Hunt, M. Jasser, F. Kainz, M. Gerz, K. Platzer and M. Platzer (eds) *Femicide: Establishing a Femicide Watch in Every Country* (pp. 42–44), Volume Vll. Vienna Liaison Office: Academic Council on the United Nations System (ACUNS). Available at: https://www.agendaforhumanity.org/sites/default/files/Femicide-Volume-VII-Establishing-a-Femicide-Watch-in-Every-Country_0.pdf

Madriaga, M. and Mallett, R. (2010). Images of criminality, victimization and disability. In S.G. Shoham, P. Knepper and M. Kett (eds) *International Handbook of Victimology*, pp. 585–610. Boca Raton, FL: CRC Press.

Maher, J.M., Spivakovsky, C., McCulloch, J., McGowan, J., Beavis, K., Lea, M., and Sands, T. (2018). Women, disability and violence: barriers to accessing justice: Final report. ANROWS Horizons, 02/2018. Sydney: ANROWS.

Matos, M. and Goncalves, M. (2019). Sleep and women intimate partner victimization: prevalence, effects and good practices in health care settings. *Sleep Science*, 12(1): 35–42.

Merry, S.E. (2016). *The Seductions of Quantification: Measuring Human Rights, Gender Violence and Sex Trafficking*. Chicago, IL: The University of Chicago Press.

Nixon R. (2011). *Slow Violence and the Environmentalism of the Poor*. Boston, MA: Harvard University Press.

Office for National Statistics (2016). Homicide compendium. Available at: https://www.ons.gov.uk/peoplepopulationandcommunity/crimeandjustice/compendium/focusonviolentcrimeandsexualoffences/yearendingmarch2015/chapter2homicide

Pease, B. (2019). *Facing Patriarchy: Overcoming a Violent Gender Order*. London: Zed Books.

Pierobom de Avila, T. (2018). The criminalisation of femicide. In K. Fitz-Gibbon, S. Walklate, J. McCulloch and J.M. Maher (eds) *Intimate Partner Violence, Risk and Security: Securing Women's Lives in a Global World*, pp. 181–198. London: Routledge.

Porter, T.M. (1996). *Trust in Numbers: The Pursuit of Objectivity in Science and Public Life* Princeton, NJ: Princeton University Press.

Radford, J. and Russell, D. (1992). *Femicide: The Politics of Woman Killing*. Buckingham: Open University Press.

Russell, D. (2001). Defining femicide and related concepts. Femicide in global perspective. speech given at the UN Symposium on Femicide, Vienna, Australia, November 2001. www.dianarussell.com/f/Defining_Femicide_-_United_Nations_Speech_by_Diana_E._H._Russell_Ph.D.pdf

Secretariat G.D. (2011). *Global Burden of Armed Violence 2011*. Cambridge: Cambridge Books.

Sheehy, E.A. (2018). Criminalizing torture as a feminist strategy: thinking through the implications. In K. Fitz-Gibbon, S. Walklate, J. McCulloch and J.M. Maher (eds) *Intimate Partner Violence, Risk and Security; Securing Women's Lives in a Global World*, pp. 255–268. London: Routledge.

Sherman, L.W. and Harris, H.M. (2015). Increased death rates of domestic violence victims from arresting vs. warning suspects in the Milwaukee Domestic Violence Experiment (MilDVE). *Journal of Experimental Criminology*, 11: 1. doi:10.1007/s11292-014-9203-x.

Small Arms Survey. (2016). A gendered analysis of violent deaths. Small Arms Survey Research Note 63. Available at: http://www.smallarmssurvey.org/fileadmin/docs/H-Research_Notes/SAS-Research-Note-63.pdf

Smith, S.G., Fowler, K.A., and Niolon, P.H. (2014). Intimate partner homicide and corollary victims in 16 states: national violent death reporting system, 2003–2009. *American Journal of Public Health*, 104(3): 461–466.

Stockl, H., Devries, K., Rotstein, A., Abrahams, N., Campbell, J., Watts, C., et al. (2013). The global prevalence of intimate partner homicide: a systematic review. *Lancet*, 382(9895): 859–865.

Telesur. (2016). Mexico: Impunity high as femicide memorial remembers victims. 15 March 2016. Available at: www.telesurenglish.net/news/Mexico-Impunity-High-as-Femicide-Memorial-Remembers-Victims-20160315-0020.html

Vives-Cases, C., Goicolea, I., Hernández, A., Sanz-Barbero, B., Gill, A.K., Baldry, A.C., et al. (2016). Expert opinions on improving femicide data collection across Europe: a concept mapping study. *PLoS ONE*, 11(2): e0148364. doi:10.1371/journal.pone.0148364

Walby, S. and Olive, P. (2014). Estimating the costs of gender-based violence in the European Union European Institute for Gender Equality. Available at: www.eige.europa.eu.

Walby, S., Towers, J., Balderston, S., Corradi, C., Francis, B., Heiskanen, M., Helweg-Larsen, K., Mergaert, L., Olive, P., Palmer, C., Stockl, H., and Strid, S. (2017) *The Concept and Measurement of Violence against Women and Men*. Bristol: Policy Press.

Walby, S. and Towers, J. (2018). Untangling the concept of coercive control: theorizing domestic violent crime. *Criminology and Criminal Justice*, 18(1): 7–28. doi:10.1177/1748895817743541

Wonders, N. (2018). Climate change, the production of gendered insecurity and slow intimate partner violence. In K. Fitz-Gibbon, S. Walklate, J. McCulloch, and J.M. Maher (eds) *Intimate Partner Violence, Risk and Security*, pp. 34–51. London: Routledge.

UN. (2014). Taking action against gender-related killing of women and girls. A/RES/68/191. Available at: https://www.unodc.org/documents/commissions/CCPCJ/Crime_Resolutions/2010-2019/2013/General_Assembly/A-RES-68-191.pdf

United Nations Women. (2011). In pursuit of justice. Progress of the world's women. Available at: www.unwomen.org/~/media/headquarters/attachments/sections/library/publications/2011/progressoftheworldswomen-2011-en.pdf

United Nations the Special Rapporteur on Violence against Women, Its Causes and Consequences (2016). Report of the Special Rapporteur on violence against women, its causes and consequences. Available at: http://undocs.org/A/71/398

Violence Policy Centre. (2012). American roulette: murder-suicide in the United States.

Waring, M. (1988). *If Women Counted: A New feminist Economics.* Toronto: Toronto Press.

Waring, M. (1999). *Counting for Nothing: What Men Value and Women Are Worth.* Toronto: Toronto Press.

Walby, S. and Towers, J. (2017). Measuring violence to end violence: mainstreaming gender. *Journal of Gender-Based Violence*, 1: 11–31. doi:10.1332/239868017

Walklate, S., McCulloch, J. Fitz-Gibbon, K., and Maher, J.M. (2019). Criminology, gender and security in the Australian context: making women's lives matter *Theoretical Criminology*, 23(1): 60–77.

World Health Organization and London School of Hygiene and Tropical Medicine. (2010). Preventing intimate partner and sexual violence against women: taking action and generating evidence, World Health Organization Geneva. Available at: www.who.int/reproductivehealth/publications/violence/9789241564007/en/

World Health Organization. (2013). Global and regional estimates of violence against women: prevalence and health effects of intimate partner violence and non-partner sexual violence.

World Health Organisation/Pan American Health Organisation. (2012). Understanding and addressing violence against women – femicide. Available at: http://apps.who.int/iris/bitstream/handle/10665/77421/WHO_RHR_12.38_eng.pdf?sequence=1

1   How do we count?

Mapping global approaches to counting women's deaths

Introduction

Efforts to 'count' the killing of women by men's violence have taken diverse forms, including the work of national death review teams, femicide censuses, and observatories. Likewise, the organizers of these efforts have been diverse, including academics, advocates, government stakeholders, and community organizations. In 2016 the United Nations (UN) called for the establishment of femicide watches or observatories in every country (ACUNS 2017, see also Simonovic 2016). These calls were made in recognition of the dearth of consistent femicide data collection globally. Despite more concerted attempts to count femicide, the data is still patchy (UNODC 2018). Evidence of the magnitude of femicide generally, and intimate femicide in particular, is relatively scarce. Few countries have specific femicide registries (Vives-Cases et al. 2016). It is critical to note that the collection of data on intimate femicide is hampered by the dearth of essential information about the victim-offender relationship; this relationship data is what constitutes this specific type of killing. One international study on intimate partner homicide found useable data in only 66 countries (out of a total of about 195 countries worldwide), with most of the available data coming from high-income countries (Stockl et al. 2013).

This chapter examines the ways in which the deaths of women killed as a consequence of intimate partner violence are presently counted across the globe. The chapter begins by examining the call by the UN Special Rapporteur for the establishment of femicide watches worldwide and considers what international data is kept and reported on femicide. It then moves on to consider country- and region-specific counting activities. The chapter then examines the rise of domestic homicide review teams/panels/networks, public femicide observatories, and femicide initiatives as well as the role of advocates and the visual memorialization of women killed.

International counts

At the international level the exercise of counting has fallen largely to the World Health Organisation (WHO), which undertakes the work, and the UN, which advocates for it. While not specifically addressing intimate femicides, the WHO has produced several key reports advancing global understandings of the nature and extent of femicide worldwide as well as some higher-level analyses of common risks of serious harm and death in the context of an intimate partner relationship (see, for example, WHO 2012, 2013). The 2013 WHO Report on the global prevalence of violence against women provides the only global data capture of the prevalence of violence against women to date. The Report (2013: 26) draws on prevalence-related studies and data since 1982 and finds that as many as 38 per cent of women murdered globally die at the hands of an intimate partner. Pointing to differences in prevalence across regions, this report highlights the significant risk of intimate partner violence faced by women in the developing world, with intimate femicide accounting for 55 per cent of femicides in the South-East Asia Region. However, this report also recognizes the difficulties of capturing data on intimate femicide in low-income settings, where even the rates of homicide are likely to be under-estimates.

In 2018, building on this work, the UN Office on Drugs and Crime (UNODC) released the Global Study on Homicide report. This study focused specifically on the gender-related killing of women and girls. It found that 58 per cent of all female homicide victims worldwide in 2017 were killed by an intimate partner or a family member (UNODC 2018). Specific to intimate femicide, in 2017 alone it is estimated that 30,000 women worldwide were killed intentionally by a current or former intimate partner. Tracking prevalence across jurisdictions, the UNODC mapped the regions where women face greater risk, though it is important to note that intimate femicide was clearly framed as a global problem – not one unique to the developing world, to low-income countries, or to any one region. Creating a global frame as a context for intimate femicide, this study found:

> women continue to bear the heaviest burden of lethal victimization as a result of gender stereotypes and inequality. Many of the victims of 'femicide' are killed by their current and former partners … the deaths of those killed by intimate partners does not usually result from random or spontaneous acts, but rather from the culmination of prior gender-related violence. Jealousy and fear of abandonment are among the motives.
>
> (UNODC 2018: 11)

It is unsurprising then that in recent years, under the leadership of the UN Special Rapporteur on violence against women, its causes and consequences, there has been a specific UN directive advocating for member states to introduce country-specific 'femicide watches' (Simonovic 2016). The benefits of the data emerging from such 'femicide watches' worldwide are succinctly captured by UNODC Deputy Executive Director, Aldo Lale-Demoz (2017), who stated 'more accurate and consistent statistics are essential to understand and respond to the nature, scope and trends of gender- related killing and related violence'.

Following the 2017 UN call, the UN Studies Association and the ACUNS Femicide Team established a Femicide Watch Platform on the Gender-Related Killing of Women and Girls. The Femicide Watch is an online platform facilitating the sharing of information about femicide (including data and statistics), as well as promoting publications, best practice examples, and collaboration between experts across the world. The Femicide Watch notes the challenges of collecting femicide data worldwide and the need to ensure that a culturally aware lens is applied to the reading of any data. It does not in and of itself undertake data collection but rather connects to and republishes the findings of other country- and region-specific watches. It is to those activities that we now turn.

National femicide observatories and monitoring programmes

Beyond the work of domestic review teams and networks, in recent years – in some cases as a direct response to the UN call for femicide watches – academics have established country- and region-specific femicide observatories. The Canadian Femicide Observatory for Justice and Accountability (CFOJA) is a country-specific example and the European Femicide Observatory is a region-specific example.

The CFOJA was launched in 2017 in response to the Special Rapporteur's call for femicide watches. Its overall mandate is to 'establish a visible and national focus on femicide in Canada' by documenting femicides as they occur and monitoring responses to these killings (Dawson 2018). The CFOJA has two express objectives:

> (1) to address the need for a single location for information about justice and accountability for femicide victims in Canada; and (2) to facilitate innovative and sustainable research agendas on femicide justice and accountability.

(CFOJA 2019)

It seeks to achieve these objectives through a range of activities, including counting all Canadian cases of femicide; documenting where femicide responses increase vulnerability and marginalization of women and girls; identifying legislation, policies, and practices that maintain the gendered structures and inequalities contributing to femicide; and facilitating exchange of information and reliable data collection.

The European Observatory of Femicide (EOF) was launched in March 2018 and is based at the University of Malta. Like the CFOJA, the EOF aims to raise awareness of femicide through a range of activities, including monitoring data, advancing research, enhancing knowledge, and cooperating with stakeholders beyond the observatory. There are, however, a range of other examples of such observatories across the globe, all taking on slightly different shapes and foci. Thus, in Latin America, in the wake of the Special Rapporteur's 2016 call for femicide watches to be established, the Ombudsman's Office committed to establishing the Latin American Femicide Observatory (LAFO), to build on the work of the pre-existing femicide register (see further Garcia 2017). In Latin America higher-level data on femicide incidents is also collected and reported by the Gender Equality Observatory for Latin America and the Caribbean (GEO).

Beyond these observatories, which are largely led and maintained by academics, under the banner of national activities, it is important to note government-run national homicide monitoring programmes/ activity taking place in some countries. Such databases often report annually and include information from police and court data about crime, violence, and homicide rates nationally (Dobash and Dobash 2015). While these datasets are typically not femicide focused per se, they often produce data relevant for comparing rates of femicide with other forms of homicide. In Australia, for example, the National Homicide Monitoring Program (NHMP) is managed by the Australian Institute of Criminology and collects data on all police-recorded homicides. Data is drawn from offence records in each Australian state and territory and state coronial records. The most recent report from the NHMP describes the nature and context of all homicides committed between July 2012 and June 2014 and was published in 2017. The recording period began in 1989, and while there is a time lag between the homicide occurring and the reporting of data, the NHMP has allowed for comparability between Australian femicide rates and other forms of homicide. The benefits and limits of big (often government run) datasets are well articulated by Dobash and Dobash (2015: 5), who state:

> A well-constructed homicide dataset contains enough information to allow for the exploration of general patterns, but it is rarely

possible to go beyond these patterns in order to reveal the complexity and dynamics of such events or to examine in any detail the different types of murder that occur such as the killing of children, older women, intimate partners, or others.

These recognized limits underlie the need for more in-depth 'counting' processes, such as those undertaken by domestic homicide review teams and networks.

Domestic homicide review teams and networks

Domestic and family homicide death reviews have been developed in numerous countries worldwide and arguably represent the most systematic and coordinated examples of counting femicides. As a model for counting deaths by family violence and identifying patterns, death reviews first emerged in the United States in the 1970s, but it was not until the 1990s that the work of death review teams extended from child deaths to the killing of women by their male intimate partners (Dawson 2013). Dawson (2013: 335) explains the impetus for their introduction:

> There were limited existing data or the capacity to collect such data that could help capture relevant and timely information needed to improve society's understandings of the individual, community, and societal factors associated with these violent lethal outcomes.

By capturing data on individual killings, death review teams operate on the premise that there is opportunity to learn from past deaths and create an evidence base to inform risk assessment practices and intervention strategies that can ultimately strengthen violence prevention initiatives (Fitz-Gibbon 2016).

In the nearly three decades since the model first emerged, there has been death review teams/networks set up in over 70 jurisdictions worldwide (Bugeja et al. 2015). These are largely established in developed rather than low-income countries (on death reviews in low-income countries, see Dawson et al. 2017). The defined scope of these teams varies significantly, making comparisons across death review reports and recommendations fraught. First, the geographical scope of these reviews varies with a small number set up nationally, while the majority are focused on a specific state, region, or territory. Second, the scope of the deaths under review and the level of data drawn upon in undertaking the review differ. In most cases death review teams rely upon, at minimum, court and police investigation data to examine domestic and family violence-related deaths, including intimate femicides. In some jurisdictions, such as New Zealand for example, the death review committee is permitted access to a significantly wider range of information about the parties involved including all relevant case files held by a range of justice, health, social service agencies (for further information, see Tolmie et al. 2017). Third, the mode and levels of reporting differ considerably, with some death review teams reporting at the individual case level while others conduct analyses across a group of cases and report findings and recommendations reflecting emerging patterns and trends. Once made, the degree to which those recommendations are followed up varies, with some teams assigning recommendations to specific agencies to take carriage of while other death review teams track recommendations to completion and/or require a written response from the relevant government stakeholder/agency (Bugeja et al. 2017).

While there is no single 'best practice' model, there is an emerging body of scholarship that examines the work of death reviews and scrutinizes the impact of these reports and recommendations (see, for example, Dawson 2017). It is argued that the best death review work is transparent, holds relevant systems and agencies to account, and therefore contributes to system changes and legislative reform (Eltringham 2013; Taylor 2008; Wilson and Websdale 2006).

The diversity of domestic violence death review work is perhaps best illustrated by looking to the United States, where this work originated and where there are between 175 and 200 review teams in operation across the 50 states (Websdale et al. 2017). In Australia, as in the United States, death reviews largely operate at the state level, whereby each jurisdiction adopts their own model, method of establishment, scope of review, and reporting requirements (see further Bugeja et al. 2013; Butler et al. 2017). In an attempt at national coordination, in 2011 the Australian Domestic and Family Violence Death Review Network (ADFVDRN) was established with the aim of producing national data of domestic and family violence-related homicides, in line with the National Plan to Reduce Violence against Women and their Children 2009–2021. The most recent report provides higher-level quantitative data on domestic and family violence homicides that occurred nationally between 2010 and 2014 (see ADFVDRN 2018). This data presents a more focused account of the circumstances of intimate femicides, the characteristics of victims and offenders, and the nature of the killing than is available through the work of the government-supported National Homicide Monitoring Program (see Cussen and Bryan 2015). It is these limitations that have driven feminist advocacy counting practices, to which we now turn.

The role of advocacy in counting

In order to address the dearth of official femicide data, activists, journalists, scholars, and women's organizations have been at the forefront of accounting for and the counting of femicides, including intimate femicide. The activism of the mothers of femicide victims and women's groups puts the killing of women and girls in Mexico on the political agenda from the 1990s, when hundreds of young women disappeared and were murdered in the small Mexican city of Juarez, near the United States' border (Livingston 2004). Such activism, including the collection of data on the number of women and girls being killed, was part of the genesis of a movement that eventually led to significant legislative changes in 16 Latin America countries (ACUNS 2017: 37–48; Pierobom de Avila 2018).

The English Femicide Census, launched in 2015, developed 'out of an urgent need to address the reality of fatal male violence against women' (Women's Aid 2018). The census, now hosted by Women's Aid, is based on information originally collected by feminist campaigner Karen Ingala Smith and recorded in her blog 'Counting Dead Women'. The database includes information on almost 1,000 women killed by men in England and Wales since 2009 (ACUNS 2017: 55–56; Smith 2018). Since 2012, similar to others inspired to count killings to fill the gap in official counts, Smith has

> searched the web for news of women killed by men; information that was hidden in plain sight-in a plethora of Domestic Homicide Reviews, police statistics, local press articles and reports in which women killed by men were mentioned.
>
> (Women's Aid 2018)

Other unofficial counts are proliferating, under the auspice of feminist activists, journalists, and scholars and spurred by the growing attention to violence against women, the UN's call to action, frustration about the continuing femicide toll, and the lag, gap, or absence of official counts.

Mirroring the UK movement 'Destroy the Joint', an Australian social media campaign was established in 2012 in response to an influential radio host's comment that 'women are destroying the joint' at the time when Australia had its first (and to date only) female prime minister (see, Gillard 2015 on gender and the prime ministership). Destroy the Joint has become most well-known for its 'counting dead women' campaign, which posts a running annual count of the number of women killed by men on a public Facebook page, comparing each year's toll to the previous year's (Caro 2013; Cullen et al. 2018; Destroy the Joint 2018). There are other similar international movements, including the Minnesota (United States) Battered Women's Coalition, which is perhaps the earliest example and publishes one of the longest running femicide reports of its kind. It has been compiling an annual femicide report for nearly 30 years (Khan and Smith 2017: 50–51). The 'Women Count USA' spreadsheet is run by Dawn Wilcox and, in line with Karen Ingala-Smith, reflects an individual advocate's desire to ensure that the lives of each individual woman killed are publicly noted (Schreyer and Health 2019).

Counting through visual memorialization

Better counting and reporting of femicides can also be seen as a form of memory justice and carried out for the purposes of memorialization. Booth (2001: 117) defines memory justice as 'the notion that the work of memory is the core of doing justice, where remembering is coupled with justice and forgetting with injustice'. Femicide counts offer a way of remembering women whose lives were violently taken, along with the social, economic, and cultural structures that support and facilitate violence against women. Ingala Smith, whose 'Counting Dead Women' became the basis of the English Femicide Census (as discussed above), states that counting

> was my way of trying to commemorate each woman, and at the same time, to say that the death of no woman killed by a man in a patriarchal society was an isolated incident.
>
> (as cited in ACUNS 2017: 55)

Many of the femicide counts that exist deliberately attend to the commemoration of individual women in ways that capture the spirit of memory-justice. The most recent report of the CFOJA, for example, contains three pages headed 'remembering…', which lists the names of all the 106 women killed in the period covered by the report as well as where they were from, if they were First Nations women or girls, and when they died (Dawson 2018: 14–16). Each of these pages features an image of a burning candle alongside the names listed. In Australia, a number of the femicide counts – including Destroy the Joint's Counting Dead Women and the Red Heart Campaign (see further Dent 2018) – visually memorialize femicide victims by including photographs and short biographies of the woman killed or, as is the case with the Red

Heart Campaign, a single heart on each point of a map of Australia to visually represent the locations where women have been killed.

Counting intimate femicide, particularly where such counting attends to the memory of those killed, offers a justice dimension by 'making past crimes visible in the present' (Booth 2006: 117). This is particularly true of intimate femicide memorials, which have a physical presence in public space. For example, in Milan (Italy), 'Il Muro Di Bambole' ('The Wall of Dolls') was built in 2014 to highlight the costs of men's violence against women. The wall is a public art installation, originally set up during Fashion Week but now a permanent feature of the streetscape, whereby dolls have been fixed to a wall to represent women who have suffered from men's violence. As explained by Anderson (2016):

> Each doll represents the place of women in a male-dominated world: the toys of men who face intimidation and violence. This is a powerful example of art being used by women to reclaim the public sphere which, due to derogatory behaviors such as catcalling, can often feel unsafe for many women.

In addition to dolls, in recent years photos of women killed by men have been added to the wall as well as lists of the rates of violence against women.

Another example of the visualization of femicide counts is the 'red shoes' movement, begun in Mexico in September 2009 and since replicated in several areas across the United States, Canada, Latin America, and Europe (Chauvet 2017). Originally set up as an art installation by Elina Cauvet to denounce decades of killing of women in Juarez, displays of red shoes have become a global symbol to represent women killed by men's violence (or in some cases, also women victims of trafficking and non-fatal violence) and have been described as 'a silent march' and a 'collective memory' (White 2017). There are other examples of public memorials for women victims of men's violence, including red dresses hanging in trees in Canada to mark the lost lives of Canada's missing and murdered indigenous women and girls and in several different municipalities in Mexico (see further Madrigal 2017). These public memorials are particularly notable as they bring deaths, which have occurred predominately in private settings, into the public sphere. They represent a push towards a public counting of men's violence against women that seeks accountability and action through visual representation in public spaces.

As we suggested at the outset, practices of counting are always political, even if the explicit political drivers for such counts are often unacknowledged. These memorials make a contribution to making the gender-based killing of women visible as well as highlighting the inadequacy of existing femicide counts. In their evocation of women's everyday gendered lives (shoes and dresses), they remind us that it is women's living of gendered lives that creates the risks they will be killed (following Shalhoub-Kevorkian 2003). These processes of re-membering or memorializing draw on long-standing practices of feminist scholarship, activism, and advocacy. As Hirsch and Smith (2002) argue, in their special issue of *Signs, Feminism and Cultural Memory*, feminist scholarship and activism have been deeply concerned with redefining culture: its production, who participates, and what is valued. They locate memory as individual and collective and, critically for our project here, contend that memory is in the present but that it also looks to the future. In creating memorials of what has occurred, of each of the women who have been killed by male perpetrators in the past, they are also looking forward – to the cessation of such violence, to the security of all women and girls. We will return to this contention, that counts remembering and recognizing women's lives can become part of prevention in ways that exceed the technical work of counting, later in this book.

Conclusion

This chapter has documented the numerous ways in which governments, academics, and advocates have sought to 'count' intimate femicide worldwide. It has demonstrated the multiplicity of ways that one can count the killing of women but also the diversity of aims and desired outcomes sought from counting. Importantly the need to acknowledge and interrogate existing counts, both for what is included and for what is as yet unseen, remains pressing. At the time of writing, the final report of the Canadian National Inquiry into Missing and Murdered Indigenous Women and Girls (2019) was released. Repeating and reinforcing the earlier finding made in the Truth and Reconciliation Report, the Inquiry found that the killing of thousands of First Nations women in Canada in recent decades has to date been largely ignored, overlooked, and/or under investigated by authorities. This Report argues that the disappearance of these women, materially and then politically and structurally, amounts to race-based genocide (Austen and Bilefsky, 2019). As we engage with the politics of counting murdered women and note the increasing efforts to do so, it is critical to recognize that some groups of women killed continue to be invisible.

References

Academic Council on the United Nations System. (2017). *Femicide VII: Establishing a Femicide Watch in Every Country.* Vienna: ACUNS. Available at: https://acuns.org/femicide-volume-vii-establishing-a-femicide-watch-in-every-country/

Anderson, R. (2016). A brief history of Milan's street art. *Impakter.* Available at: https://impakter.com/brief-history-milans-street-art/

Austen, I. and Bilefsky, D. (2019). Canadian inquiry calls killings of indigenous women genocide. *The New York Times.* New York, United States.

Australian Domestic and Family Violence Death Review Network (ADFVRN, 2018). Australian domestic and family violence death review network – data report 2018. Domestic Violence Death Review Team.

Booth, J.W. (2001). The unforgotten: memories of justice. *American Political Science Review,* 95(4): 777–791.

Booth, J.W. (2006). *Communities of Memory: On Witness, Identity, and Justice.* Ithaca, New York: Cornell University Press.

Bugeja, L., Butler, A., Buxton, E., Ehrat, H., Hayes, M., McIntyre, S., and Walsh, C. (2013). The implementation of domestic violence death reviews in Australia. *Homicide Studies,* 17(4): 353–374.

Bugeja, L., Dawson, M., McIntyre, S.-J., and Walsh, C. (2015). Domestic/family violence death reviews: an international comparison. *Trauma, Violence, & Abuse,* 16(2): 179–187.

Bugeja, L., Dawson, M., McIntyre, S-J., and Poon, J. (2017). Domestic/family violence death reviews: an international comparison. In M. Dawson (ed). *Domestic Homicide Reviews: An International Perspective,* pp. 3–26. London: MacMillan-Palgrave.

Butler, A., et al. (2017). Australia. In M. Dawson (ed). *Domestic Homicide Reviews: An International Perspective,* pp. 125–158. London: MacMillan-Palgrave.

Canadian Femicide Observatory for Justice and Accountability. (2019). Who we are. Available at: https://femicideincanada.ca/home/who

Caro, J. ed. (2013). *Destroying the Joint: Why Women Have to Change the World.* Brisbane: University of Queensland Press.

Chauvet, E. (2017). Zapatos Rojos/Red Shoes. In *Femicide: Volume VII.* Vienna: Academic Council on the United Nations System. Available at: www.agenda forhumanity.org/sites/default/files/Femicide-Volume-VII-Establishing-a-Femicide-Watch-in-Every-Country_0.pdf

Cullen, P., Vaughan, G., Zhuoyang, L., Price, J., Yu, D., and Sullivan, E. (2018). Counting dead women in Australia: An in-depth case review of femicide. *Journal of Family Violence,* 34(1): 1–8.

Cussen, T. and Bryant, W. (2015). Domestic/family homicide in Australia, Research in Practice no. 38, Australian Institute of Criminology: Canberra.

Dawson, M. (2013). Fatality and death reviews. *Homicide Studies,* 17(4): 335–338.

Dawson, M. (ed) (2017). *Domestic Homicides and Death Reviews: An International Perspective.* London: Palgrave Macmillan.

Dawson, M. (2018). The Canadian femicide observatory for justice and accountability report. Available at: https://femicideincanada.ca

Dawson, M., Mathews, S., Abrahams, N., and Campbell, J. (2017). Death reviews in the context of domestic homicide in low to middle income countries: South Africa as a case study. In M. Dawson (ed) *Domestic Homicide Reviews: An International Perspective*, pp. 345–372. London: MacMillan-Palgrave.

Dent, G. (2018). The saddest map of Australia you will ever see. *Women's Agenda.* Available at: https://womensagenda.com.au/latest/australian-femicide-map-the-saddest-map-youll-ever-see/

Destroy the Joint. (2018). Available at: www.facebook.com/DestroyTheJoint/

Dobash, R.E. and Dobash, R.P. (2015). *When Men Murder Women*. Oxford: Oxford University Press.

Eltringham, L. (2013). Why death reviews matter. DVRCV Advocate, issue 1 (Autumn/Winter): 35–39.

Fitz-Gibbon, K. (2016). Churchill fellowship report. Canberra, Australia Capital Territory: The Winston Churchill Memorial Trust. Available at: www.churchilltrust.com.au/fellows/detail/4013/Kate+Fitz-Gibbon

Garcia, F. (2017) Argentina: Femicide registries and observatories. In *Femicide: Volume VII*. Vienna: Academic Council on the United Nations System. Available at: www.agendaforhumanity.org/sites/default/files/Femicide-Volume-VII-Establishing-a-Femicide-Watch-in-Every-Country_0.pdf

Gillard, J. (2015). *Julia Gillard: My Story*. North Sydney: Vintage Books.

Hirsch, M. and Smith, V. (2002). Feminism and cultural memory: An introduction. *Signs*, 28(1): 1–19.

Khan, S. and Smith, B. (2017). Minnesota's femicide report. In *Femicide: Volume VII*. Vienna: Academic Council on the United Nations System. Available at: www.agendaforhumanity.org/sites/default/files/Femicide-Volume-VII-Establishing-a-Femicide-Watch-in-Every-Country_0.pdf

Lale-Demoz, A. (2017). Gender-related killing affects all societies. In *Femicide: Volume VII*. Vienna: Academic Council on the United Nations System. Available at: www.agendaforhumanity.org/sites/default/files/Femicide-Volume-VII-Establishing-a-Femicide-Watch-in-Every-Country_0.pdf

Livingston, J. (2004). Murder in Juarez: Gender, sexual violence, and the global assembly line. *Frontiers: A Journal of Women Studies*, 25(1): 59–76.

Madrigal, S. (2017). La Muerte Sal por el Oriente: a collaborative artistic project about femicide in Mexico. In *Femicide: Volume VII*. Vienna: Academic Council on the United Nations System. Available at: www.agendaforhumanity.org/sites/default/files/Femicide-Volume-VII-Establishing-a-Femicide-Watch-in-Every-Country_0.pdf

Pierobom de Avila, T. (2018). The criminalisation of femicide in intimate partner violence. In K. Fitz-Gibbon, S. Walklate, J. McCulloch, and J.M. Maher (eds) *Risk and Security: Securing Women's Lives in a Global World*, pp. 181–198. Oxon, New York: Routlege.

Schreyer, N. and Health, K. (2019). A school nurse is on a mission to count the women killed by men. *The Atlantic*. February 16. Available at: www.theat lantic.com/health/archive/2019/02/building-public-database-murdered-women/582769/

Shalhoub-Kevorkian, N. (2003). Re-examining femicide: breaking the silence and crossing 'scientific' borders. *Signs: Journal of Women in Culture and Society*, 28(2): 581–608.

Simonovic, D. (2016). Report of the Special Rapporteur on violence against women, its causes and consequences, A/71/398. Available at: www.un.org/ga/search/view_doc.asp?symbol=A/71/398&Submit=Search&Lang=E

Smith, I. (2018). Counting dead women. Available at: https://kareninga lasmith.com/counting-dead-women/

Stockl, H., Devries, K., Rotstein, A., Abrahams, N., Campbell, J., Watts, C., et al. (2013). The global prevalence of intimate partner homicide: a systematic review. *The Lancet*, 382(9): 859–865.

Taylor, B. (2008). Dying to be heard: domestic and family violence death reviews: discussion paper. Queensland, Australia: Red Rose Foundation. Available at: www.redrosefoundation.com.au/wp-content/uploads/2016/09/Dying-To-be-Heard-Discussion-Paper.pdf

Tolmie, J., Wilson, D., and Smith, R. (2017). New Zealand. In M. Dawson (ed) *Domestic Homicide Reviews: An International Perspective*, pp. 159–200. London: MacMillan-Palgrave.

United Nations Office on Drugs and Crime. (2018). Global study on homicide: gender-related killing of women and girls. Vienna: United Nations Office on Drugs and Crime. Available at: www.unodc.org/documents/data-and-analysis/GSH2018/GSH18_Gender-related_killing_of_women_and_girls.pdf

Vives-Cases, C., Goicolea, I., Hernández, A., Sanz-Barbero, B., Gill, A.K., Baldry, A.C., et al. (2016). Expert opinions on improving femicide data collection across Europe: a concept mapping study. *PLoS ONE*, 11(2): e0148364. doi:10.1371/journal. pone.0148364

Websdale, N., Celaya, A., and Mayer, S. (2017). United States. In M. Dawson (ed) *Domestic Homicide Reviews: An International Perspective*, pp. 27–58. London: MacMillan-Palgrave.

White,R.(2017).Redshoesraiseawarenessaboutviolencetowardswomen.WZZM. Available at: www.wzzm13.com/article/news/local/grand-rapids-central/red-shoes-raise-awareness-about-violence-toward-women/485110877

Wilson, J.S. and Websdale, N. (2006). Domestic violence fatality review teams: an interprofessional model to reduce deaths. *Balance: Journal of the Northern Territory Law Society*, 97(3): 28–34.

Women's Aid. (2018). Femicide census: profiles of women killed by men. Available at www.womensaid.org.uk/what-we-do/campaigning-and-influencing/femicide-census/

World Health Organisation. (2012). Understanding and addressing violence against women: femicide. World Health Organization: Available at: https://

apps.who.int/iris/bitstream/handle/10665/77421/WHO_RHR_12.38_eng.
pdf?sequence=1
World Health Organization. (2013). Global and regional estimates of violence
against women: prevalence and health effects of intimate partner violence
and non-partner sexual violence, World Health Organization. Available
at: https://apps.who.int/iris/bitstream/handle/10665/85239/9789241564625_
eng.pdf?sequence=1

2 Trends in counting
What do the numbers mean?

Introduction

Building on our exploration in Chapter 1 of the different ways that intimate femicide deaths are counted, this chapter presents the figures and examines the rates of intimate femicide across the world. In doing so, the chapter is structured in five parts. The first two sections briefly scan global and country-level data on intimate femicide prevalence, noting how countries compare within and across regions. We then turn to consider which femicides are not visible in these official counts, focusing on three specific contexts of femicide – honour killings, dowry-related deaths, and the killing of indigenous women and girls. In the final two sections of the chapter, we examine how the introduction of new femicide laws across Latin America has contributed to the official counting of intimate femicide, and lastly, we briefly consider what the rates of intimate femicide reveal in terms of the level of risk that women face. In doing so, at the outset of this chapter we acknowledge significant body of work that notes the underreporting of all forms of violence against women, including intimate partner violence (see, inter alia, Felson et al. 2006; UNODC 2018: 42). Interestingly, the underreporting of violence against women has been noted in both the developed and the developing world (UNODC 2018, see also Palermo et al. 2013), and in some regions, recognition of the low levels of official reporting and responses to the killing of women has energized law reform to introduce a dedicated offence of femicide/feminicide (as touched on in Chapter 1 and further explored in the latter half of this chapter).

Global intimate femicide rate

Intimate femicide is recognized globally as a leading cause of death among women (Black 2018; Garcia-Morena et al. 2005; Manjoo 2012; UNODC 2018). This has been a consistent finding for over 25 years.

More recently a 2018 study by the UNODC found that in 2017 alone 30,000 women worldwide were 'intentionally killed' by a current or former intimate partner (UNODC 2018: 10). At the regional level this equates to 11,000 women killed by a male intimate partner in both Asia and Africa, 6,000 women in the Americas, 2,000 in Europe, and 200 in Oceania (UNODC 2018: 10). When the rate per 100,000 of the population of women killed by their intimate partner is considered, the UNODC (2018: 11) study reveals that in 2017 Africa had the highest rate of women killed by an intimate partner: 1.7 per 100,000 of the female population. This was followed by the Americas (1.2), Oceania (0.9), Europe (0.6), and Asia (0.5). The global rate of intimate femicide for 2017 was cited at 1.3 per 100,000 of the female population (UNODC 2018: 11). This global rate is marginally lower than that cited for 2012, where the rate of women killed by an intimate partner per 100,000 of the population was 1.4 (UNODC 2013).

UN Women has developed a Global Database on Violence against Women as well as a Virtual Knowledge Centre to End Violence against Women and Girls. This seeks to document the initiatives of the UN to address violence against women and presents information on the prevalence of different forms of violence against women across the UN member states. Attempts have also been made to understand the economic cost of violence against women, intimate femicide included (Centers for Disease Control and Prevention 2003; Walby 2004; WHO 2004). There is less data available on the economic cost of violence against women in low- and middle-income countries (Bugeja et al. 2017: 4).

National intimate femicide rates

The opening paragraph of this book briefly presented some of the national figures of women killed by their male intimate partners around the world. Here we look to these numbers in more detail. While rates of intimate femicide have remained relatively stable in most countries, research from the last five years has found that in the United States, the prevalence rates have risen in the period since 2014 (Black 2018; Fridel and Fox 2019; see also Cooper and Smith 2011). Of female homicide victims in the United States, over 60 per cent are killed by a male intimate partner (Violence Policy Center 2018). This figure, however, does not include women killed by an ex-boyfriend, as the FBI does not collate data on this category. This practice distinguishes it from data collected on intimate femicides in several other countries and means that the total figure cited above is an underestimate of women killed by current and former partners. The frequency of intimate femicide, as is the case more generally for all homicides in the United States, is often attributed to availability of, and presence of, firearms in the home (see, inter alia, Fridel and Fox 2019; Violence Policy Center 2018), though the extent to which this constitutes an explanation for these figures is clearly debatable (see further Chapter 5). Further figures are also worth noting. The high rates of women killed in Mexico over the past two decades are significant (see further WHO 2012); however, it is difficult to estimate what percentage of those women killed are victims of intimate partner femicide. In Canada, the Canadian Femicide Observatory for Justice and Accountability (CFOJA) reports that on average one woman is killed every week by her male partner in Canada (Dawson 2018). Like in other countries, intimate partner homicide is the most common type of femicide, accounting for 31 per cent of all homicides involving a female victim (Dawson 2018: 8).

To look beyond North America, in Australia it is estimated that one woman is killed every week by a current or former partner (State of Victoria 2014). In New Zealand *The Homicide Report*, a recently produced publicly searchable homicide database, found that between 2004 and 2019, intimate femicides account for one in eight homicides in New Zealand and half of all homicides involving a female homicide victim over the age of 18 years old. In the UK the work of Women's Aid and Karen Ingala-Smith through the Femicide Census has been central to informing understandings of the killing of women. In their most recent report, it was recorded that between 2009 and 2017 in the UK a woman was killed every four days by a current or former male intimate partner (Long et al. 2018). Of those women a third were killed in the period immediately following relationship separation.

Intimate femicide data has been collated more regularly over the last ten years in Europe, coinciding with the formatting and emerging work of the Femicide across Europe COST Network (see further, Corradi et al. 2018: 93–94). In 2007, Project DAPHNE (2007) found that there were approximately 3,500 deaths relating to intimate partner violence every year across Europe, of which more than 77 per cent involved female victims. In the decade since Project Daphne, some researchers have pointed to an increase in the total number of women killed (see, for example, Spinelli 2011). Within Europe, the UNODC (2018) provided some country-level data, which reveals a higher-than-average risk of intimate femicide for women living in Albania, Croatia, Hungary, and Lithuania in comparison with other countries in the region.

National estimates across Asian and African countries are less readily available; however, the UNODC (2018) global study found that African women are at the highest global risk of intimate partner homicide, citing 1.7 victims of intimate femicide per 100,000 of the female population. Other studies find similarly high rates of intimate femicide across Africa (see, inter alia, Abrahams et al. 2009). In Asia, while the total number of deaths is comparatively on par with the number of women killed by a male intimate partner in Africa, when considered as a rate per 100,000 of the population, Asian women are the least likely globally to be killed by a male intimate partner. The UNODC (2018) cited a rate of 0.5 per 100,000 of the population.

Finally, the high rates of intimate femicide across Latin American countries have garnered significant attention in recent years and contributed to the introduction of new criminal laws designed to improve the recording of, and investigation into, femicide offences (as discussed below). Latin America has the highest homicide rate in the world (Avila 2018; Forero 2018), and as such, it is perhaps unsurprising that it also records significant rates of intimate partner killing. With the exception of El Salvador and Honduras, intimate femicides are the most common type of femicide (Gender Equality Observation for Latin America and the Caribbean (GEOLAC) 2018). Described as an 'epidemic' in intimate homicides, this epidemic results in the death of approximately four women each day in Brazil (Pierobom de Avila 2018). When the incident rates are considered per 100,000 women in the population, the prevalence of intimate homicide ranges from 1.98 in the Dominican Republic to 0.47 in Chile (these rates are based on 2017 data; see further GEOLAC 2018).

Unreported and unrecorded intimate femicides

> Femicide thrives in silence. Violence against women is almost universally under-reported, irrespective of a country's development or wealth. Women and girls are reluctant to report violence due to fear of reprisal and stigmatization or economic and psychological dependence. If they do report, they're often intimidated into silence, told that their case will be discredited or deemed a private matter.
>
> (Black 2018)

Beyond country-level data, there are intimate femicides with particular characteristics that are less likely to be captured in official statistics and prevalence rates and thus are often invisibilized, particularly where they are perpetrated in developing countries. Two examples, while not exclusively constituting intimate femicide (in that family members may also be implicated in the killing), are dowry-related killings and so-called 'honour' killings. We briefly explore each of these in turn here before examining the underreporting and recording of femicides involving an indigenous victim.

The dowry-related killing of women refers to killings where a woman or girl is 'killed or driven to commit suicide after being subjected to continuous harassment and abuse by the groom's family in an effort to extort dowry payment or increased dowry involving cash and goods' (UNODC 2018: 32). In their 2018 global study, the UNODC reported that while a range of counties have introduced legislation to ban the practice of dowry, it continues to be practiced (potentially due to religious and/or cultural traditions). As noted by the former Special Rapporteur on Violence against Women, its causes and its consequences, Rashida Manjoo (2012: 15):

> Despite legislative reforms, dowry is an indispensable part of weddings in this region [South Asia]; it has been a cause of violence against women, and the laws have failed to have an impact in curbing dowry or elevating the status of women within marriage.

As such, and while specific prevalence rates are difficult to determine, the practice of dowry-related killing is noted in several countries worldwide, particularly in South-East Asia and India (Manjoo 2012; UNODC 2018). In India, for example, it is estimated that 8,233 young women were killed in a dowry-related killing in 2012 alone (Nelson 2013). Importantly in the context of this analysis of those 8,233 cases, only 32 per cent resulted in a criminal conviction, highlighting the significant barriers to justice that are faced (Nelson 2013). It also means that the majority of femicides occurring in this context are unlikely to be recorded in criminal justice statistics.

Another example of femicides likely to be invisible in official prevalence rates is honour-related killings (Manjoo 2012: 12). Whilst the term 'honour killing' is itself subject to contestation, as explained by Manjoo (2012: 13), 'United Nations treaty bodies have expressed concerns that honour-related crimes often go unreported, are rarely investigated and usually go unpunished'. In agreement, the High Commission for Human Rights Navi Pillay (2010) has also previously stated:

> The reality for most victims, including victims of honour killings, is that State institutions fail them and that most perpetrators of domestic violence can rely on a culture of impunity for the acts they commit – acts which would often be considered as crimes, and be punished as such, if they were committed against strangers

Typically perpetrated by the family members of a young female victim, but may be committed with the victim's male intimate partner, the UNODC (2018: 31) defines honour-related killings as the killing of a woman or girl by family members where 'they consider that the behaviour of female family members has brought shame on the family and needs to be sanctioned' (see also DeKeseredy and Hall-Sanchez 2018; Faqir 2001; Khafagy 2005). Prevalence data on honour killings is patchy as the killings are often unreported, unrecorded, and/or miscategorized (UNODC 2018).

The Asian Development Bank (ADB) and UN Women (2018: 111) found that the prevalence of honour killings is 'particularly high' in Afghanistan and Pakistan, where a 'culture of impunity' has meant that cases are often misrepresented in official counts as accidental deaths, if reported at all. We do note though that over the last ten years, there have been efforts worldwide to improve the reporting and recording of honour killings (see, for example, Afghanistan Independent Human Rights Commission 2013), and as such, they are now more likely than previously to be included within some national death counts.

Beyond these two particular types of intimate femicide, research has consistently noted that Aboriginal and Indigenous women are significantly overrepresented as victims of intimate femicide (see, inter alia, Amnesty International 2009; Boyce 2016; Dawson 2018; Manjoo 2012; Romero et al. 2017) but potentially invisible in official data and prevalence rates. This is most clearly captured in the findings of the recent *Canadian National Inquiry into Missing and Murdered Indigenous Women*, which highlighted the systemic killing of indigenous women as well as the significant underreporting and recording of these victims (National Inquiry into Missing and Murdered Indigenous Women and Girls 2019, hereinafter the 'Inquiry'). Making 230 recommendations, this Inquiry concluded that the murder and deliberate disappearance of Indigenous women and girls across Canada – including those killed within and outside of intimate partner relationships – amounted to genocide (on the Report's findings, see further, Moss 2019). The Inquiry (2019: 3) endeavoured to 'gather all of the truths' surrounding the systemic killing and disappearance of indigenous women and girls in Canada; however, capturing the gravity of the task at hand, it concluded:

> no one knows an exact number of missing and murdered Indigenous women, girls and 2SLGBTQQIA people in Canada. Thousands of women's deaths or disappearances have likely gone unrecorded over the decades, and many families likely did not feel

ready or safe to share with the National Inquiry ... We do know that thousands of Indigenous women, girls and 2SLGBTQQIA have been lost to the Canadian genocide to date.

As reflected above, the recent Canadian inquiry brings to the fore questions surrounding whose deaths counts and in particular the challenges posed by attempts to reverse the silencing of women's deaths. Since the release of the Canadian Inquiry Final Report, attention has been turned in other countries to the disappearance and killing of Indigenous women and girls, including in the United States, where there are now calls for an investigation akin to that recently completed in Canada (Golden 2019; Moss 2019). The lack of will, or perhaps the willingness to overlook, the killing of indigenous women for decades in these countries, raises multiple questions of relevance to exercises 'to count'. In how many other countries do the intimate femicide rates significantly underrepresent and fail to capture the Indigenous lives lost to intimate partner violence? To what degree is this a failure to acknowledge the deaths of these women and, in doing so, a failure to adequately acknowledge their lives? And perhaps most pertinent to this book's exploration, how now can this be remedied? Or perhaps in acknowledging that this injustice may never be remedied, how can stakeholders, advocates, and academics work together moving forward to better 'count' and 'account' for the lives of indigenous women killed by intimate partner violence?

Feminicide across Latin America: changing what 'counts' through law reform

In response to mounting concerns that the killing of women was overlooked, unrecorded, and responded to in many cases, there has been a push across Latin America and the Caribbean in recent years for countries to introduce a specific offence of femicide. The justification being that the creation of a specific law would flag all cases where a woman is murdered because of her sex (Dawson 2015) while also challenging the culture of impunity that has traditionally surrounded the killing of women. Across Latin America and the Caribbean in the ten-year period between 2007 and 2017, 18 countries have introduced a criminal offence of femicide (Essayag 2017; GEOLAC 2018), including Brazil (*Act No 13.104 (2015)*) (*Feminicide Law*) (see further Pierobom de Avila 2018), Argentina (in 2012), Bolivia (in 2013), Chile (in 2010), Colombia (in 2015), Guatemala (in 2008), Mexico (in 2012), and Peru (in 2013) (see further, UNODC 2018: Annex). In total this equates to just under half (48 per cent) of all countries in the region (Essayag 2017).

While they are often grouped together under the broad heading of 'femicide/feminicide' laws, there are key differences in the definitions applied as to what 'counts' as femicide in each of the aforementioned countries. Some countries, for example, have restricted the legislation to apply only to women killed by an intimate partner (see, for example, Chile and Dominican Republic) or the killing of women by an intimate partner and/or a family member (see Brazil). In other cases, while still termed 'feminicide', the legislation captures a significantly wider range of gender-based killings, including the killing of a pregnant woman (see, for example, Bolivia, Peru, Panama), a woman for the purpose of trafficking in persons (see, for example, Peru), a woman subject to sexual violence prior to the killing (see, for example, Costa Rica, Paraguay, Honduras), a woman in the presence of her children (see, for example, Ecuador, Guatemala, Panama), or the killing of a woman by a state official (see, for example, El Salvador). The drafting of the legislation is important in that it dictates what comes to be known, counted, and labelled as 'femicide/feminicide' within that country. While there are these differences in the specifics of the legislation in each country, the emergence of femicide laws has undoubtedly played an important role in the counting of intimate femicides as they have increased awareness of the killing of women and girls in relevant countries (Weil and Naudi 2018) and also enhanced the official recording of these deaths.

Understanding the level of risk

For nearly a decade the UNODC Global Study on Homicide has consistently found that women worldwide are at a far greater risk of intimate partner homicide than their male counterparts (see, inter alia, 2011, 2013, 2018). This gendered pattern in prevalence is also reported in country-specific studies. In the United States, for example, it is estimated that men commit approximately double the number of intimate partner homicides as their female counterparts (Websdale 2017: 31). Similar patterns are evident elsewhere. In Latin America, it is estimated that females are killed by a male intimate partner at a rate five times higher than males killed by a female intimate partner (UNODC 2018: 21). In Europe, 2016 data indicated that intimate femicide was four times more prevalent than intimate partner homicides involving a male victim (UNODC 2018: 21).

When considered alongside other forms of femicide, the UNODC Global Study found that a third of female homicide victims worldwide in 2017 were killed by a male intimate partner, amounting to a global prevalence rate of 0.8 per 100,000 of the population (UNODC 2018).

At a country-specific level, in the United States, for example, research has found that homicides involving a female killed by a stranger account for only 10 per cent of homicides nationally (Catalano et al. 2009), and in Canada, it is reported that approximately 16 per cent of femicides involve a female victim who is unknown to the perpetrator (Dawson 2018). Likewise, in the UK, the Femicide Census found that in 2017 just over 20 per cent (21.6) of femicides involved a stranger unknown to the victim, while 46 per cent of homicides involved a woman who had been in a current or former intimate partner relationship (Long et al. 2018). These statistics – which mirror similar patterns in Australia and New Zealand – reveal that while there are some variances in the specific rate of intimate femicide and stranger femicide across countries and regions, in the majority of nations worldwide, women face the greatest risk of femicide from their current or former male intimate partners. The relationship between risk, counting, and the role of intervention is explored more fully in Chapter 5 and Conclusion.

Conclusion

This chapter has explored the data that exists on the killing of women by their male intimate partners. While there are variances in the degree of data collected and definitions of what 'counts' as intimate femicide within and across different jurisdictions, there are increasingly country- and region-level data reported on annual femicide rates, which assist in efforts towards 'counting'. There are some intimate femicides, however, that are less visible in these counts. The gravity of the failure to 'count' and 'account for' the killing of a woman is well captured by the UN Secretary General, who, in 2006, stated:

> Impunity for violence against women compounds the effects of such violence as a mechanism of control. When the State fails to hold the perpetrators accountable, impunity not only intensifies the subordination and powerlessness of the targets of violence, but also sends a message to society that male violence against women is both acceptable and inevitable. As a result, patterns of violent behaviour are normalized.

This rings particularly true in the current context, where the systemic invisibilization of the killing of indigenous women and girls has been bought to the fore in Canada, an awakening that may well have ripple effects to other countries where the disappearance of indigenous women has failed to be investigated and accounted for.

References

Abrahams, N., Jewkes, R., Martin, L.J., Mathews, S., Vetten, L., and Lombard, C. (2009). Mortality of women from intimate partner violence in South Africa: a national epidemiological study. *Violence and Victims*, 24(4): 546–556.

Afghanistan Independent Human Rights Commission. (2013). National inquiry report on: factors and causes of rape and honour killing in Afghanistan. Afghanistan Independent Human Rights Commission, Kabul, Afghanistan.

Amnesty International. (2009). No more stolen sisters: the need for a comprehensive response to discrimination and violence against Aboriginal Women. September. Amnesty International. Available at: www.amnesty.org/en/library/info/AMR20/012/2009/en

Asian Development Bank and UN Women. (2018). Gender equality and the sustainable development goals in Asia and the Pacific: baseline and pathways for transformative change by 2030. Asian Development Bank and UN Women, Bangkok, Thailand.

Avila, T.P. (2018). Facing domestic violence against women in Brazil: advances and challenges. *International Journal of Crime, Justice and Social Democracy*, 7(1): 15–29.

Black, M. (2018). Violence against women is an issue that concerns us all. *UNICEF USA*. December 10. Available at: www.unicefusa.org/stories/violence-against-women-issue-concerns-us-all/35247

Boyce, J. (2016). Victimization of aboriginal people in Canada, 2014. Ministry of Industry, Statistics Canada.

Bugeja, L., Dawson, M., McIntyre, S., and Poon, J. (2017). Domestic/family violence death reviews: an international comparison. In M. Dawson (ed) *Domestic Homicides and Death Reviews: An International Perspective*, pp. 3–26. London: Palgrave Macmillan.

Catalano, S., Smith, E., Snyder, H., and Rand, E. (2009). Female victims of violence: Bureau of justice statistics: selected findings. Bureau of Justice Statistics. Available at: www.bjs.gov/content/pub/pdf/fvv.pdf

Centres for Disease Control and Prevention. (2003). Costs of intimate partner violence against women in the United States. National Centre for Injury Prevention and Control, Atlanta, Georgia.

Cooper, A. and Smith, E.L. (2011). Homicide trends in the United States: 1980–2008. Bureau of Justice Statistics. Available at: www.bjs.gov/content/pub/pdf/htus8008.pdf

Corradi, C., Baldry, A.C., Buran, S., Kouta, C., Schrottle, M., and Stevkovic, L. (2018). Exploring the data on femicide across Europe. In S. Weil, C. Corradi, and M. Naudi (eds) *Femicide across Europe: Theory, Research and Prevention*, pp. 93–166. Bristol: Policy Press.

Dawson, M. (2015). Punishing femicide: criminal justice responses to the killing of women over four decades. *Current Sociology*, 64(7): 996–1016.

Dawson, M. (2018). *106* women and girls killed by violence: eight-month report by the Canadian femicide observatory for justice and accountability. Canadian Femicide Observatory for Justice and Accountability: University of Guelph, Canada. Available at: https://femicideincanada.ca/sites/default/files/201809/CFOJA%20FINAL%20REPORT%20ENG%20V3.pdf

DeKeseredy, W. and Hall-Sanchez, A. (2018). Male violence against women in the Global South: what we know and what we don't know. In K. Carrington, R. Hogg, J. Scott, and M. Sozzo (eds) *The Palgrave Handbook of Criminology and the Global South*, pp. 883–900. Switzerland: Springer.

Essayag, S. (2017). From commitment to action: policies to end violence against women in Latin America and the Caribbean: regional analysis document. United Nations Development Programme and UN Women, Panama.

Faqir, F. (2001). Intrafamily femicide in defence of honour: the case of Jordan. *Third World Quarterly*, 22(1): 65–82.

Felson, R., Messner, S.F., Hoskin, A., and Deane, G. (2006). Reasons for reporting and not reporting domestic violence to the police. *Criminology*, 40(3): 617–648.

Forero, J. (2018). Women in Latin America are being murdered at record rates. *The Wall Street Journal*. December 19. Available at: www.wsj.com/articles/it-is-better-not-to-have-a-daughter-here-latin-americas-violence-turns-against-women-11545237843

Fridel, E.E. and Fox, J.A. (2019). Gender differences in patterns and trends in U.S. homicide, 1976–2017. *Violence and Gender*, 6(1). doi:10.1089/vio.2019.0005

Garcia-Moreno, C., Jansen, H., Ellsberg, M., Heise, L., and Watts, C. (2005). WHO multi-country study on women's health and domestic violence against women: initial results on prevalence, health outcomes and women's responses. World Health Organization, Geneva, Switzerland.

Gender Equality Observatory for Latin America and the Caribbean. (2018) Femicide, the most extreme expression of violence against women. Notes for Equality No. 27, United Nations Available at: https://oig.cepal.org/sites/default/files/nota_27_eng.pdf

Golden, H. (2019). 'Sister, where did you go?': the native American women disappearing from US cities. *The Guardian*. May 1. Available at: www.theguardian.com/us-news/2019/apr/30/missing-native-american-women-alyssa-mclemore

Khafagy F. (2005). Honour killing in Egypt. UN Division for the Advancement of Women, Cairo, Egypt.

Long, J., Harper, K., Harvey, H., and Smith, K.I. (2018). The femicide census: 2017 findings – annual report on UK femicides 2017. *Femicide Census*. London: Women's Aid.

Manjoo, R. (2012). Report of the Special Rapporteur on violence against women, its causes and consequences. A/HRC/20/16. United Nations General Assembly, Vienna.

Moss, M. (2019) Missing and murdered Indigenous women and girls: an epidemic on both sides of the medicine line. *The Conversation*. June 6. Available at: https://theconversation.com/missing-and-murdered-indigenous-women-and-girls-an-epidemic-on-both-sides-of-the-medicine-line-118261

National Inquiry into Missing and Murdered Indigenous Women and Girls. (2019). Executive summary of the final report. National Inquiry into Missing and Murdered Indigenous Women and Girls, Canada.

Nelson, D. (2013). Woman killed over dowry 'every hour' in India. *The Telegraph*. September 2. Available at: www.telegraph.co.uk/news/worldnews/asia/india/10280802/Woman-killed-over-dowry-every-hour-in-India.html

Palermo, T., Bleck, J., and Peterman, A. (2013). Tip of the iceberg: reporting and gender-based violence in developing countries. *American Journal of Epidemiology*, 179(5): 602–612.

Pierobom de Avila, T. (2018). The criminalization of femicide. In K. Fitz-Gibbon, S. Walklate, J. McCulloch, and J.M. Maher (eds) *Intimate Partner Violence, Risk and Security; Securing Women's Lives in a Global World*, pp. 181–198. London: Routledge.

Pillay, N. (2010). Impunity for domestic violence, 'honour killings' cannot continue – UN official. *UN News: Global Perspective, Human Stories*, 4 March.

Project Daphne. (2007). Estimation of mortality linked to intimate partner violence in Europe – IPV EU_Mortality. *Psytel*. Avaiable at: www.pystel.eu/violences.php

Romero, D.F., Estrada, V.J., Marceau, S.G., and Rice, R. (2017). *Violence against indigenous women in the Americas: final summary report*. Canadian Association for Latin American and Canadian Studies, Canada. Available at: https://poli.ucalgary.ca/manageprofile/sites/poli.ucalgary.ca.manageprofile/files/unitis/publications/1-8355408/CALACS_Virtual_Forum_Violence_against_Indigenous_Women.pdf

Spinelli, B. (2011). Femicide and feminicide in Europe: gender motivated killings of women as a result of intimate partner violence. Expert meeting on gender-motivated killings of women, convened by the Special Rapporteur on Violence against Women, its causes and consequences, Ms Rashida Manjoo. New York, United States.

State of Victoria. (2014). *Measuring the Toll: The Family Violence Index*. Victorian Government: Melbourne, Victoria.

United Nations Office on Drugs and Crime. (2011). *Global Study on Homicide*. Vienna, Austria: United Nations Office on Drugs and Crime.

United Nations Office on Drugs and Crime. (2013) *Global Study on Homicide*. Vienna, Austria: United Nations Office on Drugs and Crime.

United Nations Office on Drugs and Crime. (2018). *Global Study on Homicide: Gender-Related Killing of Women and Girls*. Vienna, Austria: United Nations Office on Drugs and Crime.

United Nations Secretary General. (2006) *In-Depth Study on All Forms of Violence against Women: Report of the Secretary-General*. A/61/122/Add.1. UN Secretary General.

Violence Policy Center. (2018). *When Men Murder Women: An Analysis of 2016 Homicide Data.* Washington: Violence Policy Center.

Walby, S. (2004). *The Cost of Domestic Violence.* London: Women and Equality Unit.

Websdale, N. (2017). Trends and patterns in intimate partner homicide. In M. Dawson (ed) *Domestic Homicides and Death Reviews: An International Perspective*, pp. 27–31. London: Palgrave Macmillan.

Weil, S. and Naudi, M. (2018) Towards a European observatory on femicide. In S. Weil, C. Corradi, and M. Naudi (eds) *Femicide across Europe: Theory, Research and Prevention*, pp. 167–174. Bristol: Policy Press.

World Health Organisation. (2004) The economic dimensions of interpersonal violence. World Health Organization, Geneva, Switzerland.

World Health Organization. (2012) Understanding and addressing violence against women: femicide. World Health Organization, Geneva, Switzerland.

3 Why counting matters

The opportunities and benefits of counting intimate femicide

Introduction

In 2013 violence against women was described by the World Health Organisation (WHO) as a violation of human rights and a public health epidemic. This statement was underpinned by the figures produced by the first systemic international review of the prevalence of violence against women (WHO 2013). This review found that gendered violence affects more than one third of all women across the world. The figures are shocking and are well deserving of the epidemic proportions label. If nothing else, these figures also carry with them significant economic costs that impact on all members of society. Speaking on 21st September 2018 the UN Assistant Secretary-General and Deputy Executive Director of UN Women, Lakshmi Puri, stated: 'research indicates that the cost of violence against women could amount to around 2 per cent of the global gross domestic product (GDP). This is equivalent to $1.5 trillion, approximately, the size of the economy of Canada.' In this sense when considered in terms of the harms done and suffered, understanding the extent of the problems to be addressed, and the economic costs incurred, the recognition of the pervasive nature of such violence, and the associated violation of human rights represents, is a victory of types. Violence against women is commonly denied, minimized, and widely tolerated as an expression of male entitlement (see inter alia Dekeseredy et al. forthcoming). The figures cited in the WHO Report and elsewhere make violence against women by men more visible and in doing so may make it more difficult to maintain common attitudes of indifference that permeate so many levels of culture, society, and politics.

The 'Setting the Scene' introduction outlined the social and political significance of intimate partner violence and intimate femicide as the most extreme expression of such violence. Statistics on the number of women and children harmed by intimate partner violence, the current tallies of the number of intimate femicides in single jurisdictions, at the national level as well as globally, and the proportion of femicides and all homicides that these figures represent were laid out in Chapter 2 to underline the prevalence and enormous and tragic costs of men's violence. Building on Chapter 1's exploration of the different techniques and ambitions of counting, this chapter considers the advantages of counting intimate femicides in ways that will allow for more accurate comparison between jurisdictions and countries, the measurement of trends across time and place, and the provision of a more accurate global count. While focusing on the advantages and opportunities of counting, we do not mean to suggest these advantages will necessarily be realized or that there are not potential disadvantages and risks. Rather the advantages are given careful consideration in order to ensure we are fully conscious of the potential utility of counting as a tool aimed at ending violence against women. Chapters 4 and 5 consider the potential costs and limits of counting in relation to the ultimate goal of preventing violence against women.

The advantage of more comprehensive, more accurate, more systematic, and more consistent counting of intimate femicides includes the symbolic power of being counted as a reflection and reinforcement of the value of 'every body' (see UN General Declaration Secretariat 2015). Consistent with this, political action and investment of resources in the enhanced counting of intimate femicides, where statistics on untimely deaths are understood as part of social accounting for lives (Bayatrizi 2009), might also be a means of capturing, demonstrating, and advancing the political momentum towards the goal of ending violence against women and girls. The regular and systematic counting of, and reporting on, intimate femicides has the potential to transform the tragedy of individual women's violent deaths, by harnessing the weight of numbers to demonstrate a gendered pattern of violence in ways that implicate the gendered stratified structure of society, underpinning intimate femicide. It offers 'memory-justice' too, wherein not forgetting, particularly in the face of denial or silence about harm, violence, and culpability, might be seen as a significant expression of justice (Booth 2001). Counting intimate femicides is a way of keeping the cost of lives taken violently in circumstances where gender and intimacy are central visible in the present. These costs are not purely economic. They are costs that devalue all women's lives, and those of their children, and cast huge doubts on the wider embrace of the principles of human rights. Action beyond this counting is critical for building an evidence base for the interrelated tasks of developing, testing, and applying the theoretical frameworks and associated social changes needed to better prevent future acts of intimate femicide.

To this end, the primary purpose of the pursuit of better counting of intimate femicides is ultimately the prevention of these crimes and the transformation of society to support the end to violence against women and girls. While effective prevention is a complex and multi-faceted endeavour, intimate femicides have long been recognized as the most preventable types of homicide because histories of abuse often provide some clear indicators of risk (Bugeja et al 2013; Dearden and Jones 2008; Virueda and Payne 2010). As stated by Cullen et al. (2018), femicide is

> associated with modifiable risk factors, including previous violence and mental health issues, which represents opportunities for early intervention settings as practitioners are well-placed to identify risk and provide support. In line with recommendations for multi-sectoral approach, future research should target identification of risk and protective factors, and improved coordination of data collection.
>
> (Cullen et al. 2018)

While there is great interest in risk factors related to intimate partner violence, and particularly in indicators of potentially lethal violence as Chapter 5 sets out, projects and programmes setting out to measure and manage the risk of intimate partner violence have not readily translated into femicide prevention.

Counting matters

Over centuries feminists in all walks of life, including scholars and activists, have sought to expose and challenge male violence, particularly intimate partner violence, as the most common type of violence against women (for an early example, see Cobbe's 'Wife Torture in England' 1878). Largely as a result of these historical and ongoing efforts, there has been increased accounting for such violence, with a growing body of research on the prevalence, impacts, and costs of men's violence (Watts and Zimmerman 2002). These accountings include attempts to quantify the financial costs to national economies (see, for example, Price Waterhouse Coopers 2015 on the Australian costs) and the world economy (Hoeffler and Fearon 2015); attempts to measure the health impacts to women of intimate partner violence against other health risks (Webster 2016); and an increase in the number of femicide and intimate femicide counts being undertaken at local, regional, national, and supranational levels. Increasing attention to measuring the prevalence, impacts, and costs of intimate partner violence across a number of indicators, including intimate femicide, reflects and reinforces awareness about such violence and potentially adds to the political will and community drive to better prevent and respond to it.

Counting or measuring is one way of knowing. Quantification uses 'numbers to describe social phenomena in countable and measurable terms' (Merry 2016: 1). As Merry (2016: 19) points out, what is counted and systems of measurement, though linked to the 'myth of objectivity', are to a significant extent determined by opaque politics and values. Merry underlines the limits of quantification as a means of knowing, with a particular focus on human rights and gender violence. Her book, as its title suggests – *The Seductions of Quantification* – is a cautionary tale about reliance on quantification as an accurate measure of the nature, extent, and trends in these areas and more generally. However, much of what she writes underpins the value of counting as a way of challenging the status quo about who and what counts. She argues counting produces and constitutes a form of power. In this Merry follows Foucault in understanding knowledge-power as an integrated concept, with each aspect mutually reinforcing and intrinsically linked (see, for example, Foucault 1977). She concludes that '[n]ot all that should be counted is counted, nor does counting itself necessarily provide an accurate picture of a situation or its explanation' (Merry 2016: 220). She argues that to overcome these limits, qualitative evidence should be used along with quantitative indicators and research (Merry 2016: 222; see also Weil and Kouta 2017 on the importance of qualitative approaches to understanding femicide). We agree with Merry's insights about the limits of quantification. The risks of counting intimate femicides are explored further in Chapter 4.

However, Merry's call for greater transparency in the way quantitative measures are constructed need not deter us from counting. Such critiques might be seen to encourage us to be explicit in the values underpinning what and how we choose to count, the limits and inadequacy of counting as a primary source of knowledge, and the outcomes we hope to generate or contribute to through such counting. A keen awareness of the inevitable imbrication of knowledge and power is a call to action as much as a caution. Foucault notes that power is dynamic and that it always coexists with resistance against dominant ways of knowing (see, for example, Foucault 1977: 285). What is seen to count, the counting that takes place, and the knowledge produced tend to reflect intersecting social hierarchies grounded in lived differences of race, class, and gender, as well as diverse sexualities, ethnicities, and (dis)abilities that interact and may amplify oppressions and violence (see, for example, Crenshaw 1989 on intersectionality). Social movements of all types, including women's movements, have frequently sought to challenge such hierarchies by refusing to accept the diminished social and political status attached to not being counted. The phrase 'stand up and be counted' points to the sense of collective action and the demand to be seen and heard, associated with the idea of making a difference or a change through being counted.

What and who counts matters

Counting or being counted carries at least two broad meanings – one points to calculation and numbers, the other to the weight, importance, and/or significance of a matter or person. These two meanings intersect. For a person or issue not to be counted can be read as not counting in the sense that the what or who that is not counted does not matter and is not important and/or significant. For this reason, counting is widely considered a precondition to social change, so changing social conditions and addressing social problems requires first that the problem is identified and understood by being quantified. Baytrizi (2009) argues that the practices of counting the dead emerging in the seventeenth century reflected increased attention to social patterns, problems, and indeed the governance of social life itself. In relation to crime in particular it is argued that 'unless there is accurate and comparable data collection on a given crime, there will be no proper understanding of it and no effective strategy with which to combat it' (ACUNS 2017).

There are many examples of the significance of counting as a mark of human rights and as a vehicle for social change and social justice. In Australia, for example, a referendum in 1967 led to the federal constitution being amended to remove a heading that "Aborigines not to be counted in reckoning population" and the underlying section which read:

> In reckoning the numbers of the people of the Commonwealth, or of a State or other part of the Commonwealth, aboriginal natives shall not be counted (section 127).

It is a widely held myth that the referendum gave Australia's First Nations peoples citizenship and the right to vote. That so many people falsely believed being counted in the national census bestowed citizenship rights suggests the power of counting as a symbol of political and legal rights, as well as the necessity of explaining exactly what it is each count means. Beyond symbolic value, the demographic data collected in the census after the referendum provided an evidence base for government policy and in particular enabled the determination and monitoring of key health indicators (Gardiner-Garden 2007). More than 50 years later, the significant health gap between Indigenous and non-Indigenous Australians still exists and in many respects is widening (Department of Prime Minister and Cabinet 2019). This is a dramatic demonstration that counting alone is not enough to create the desperately needed social change. The referendum in 1967 was important symbolically and provided an evidence base to quantify the gap in health outcomes between First Nations people and others. The political will to address the myriad and compounding injustices that underpin and maintain the continuing history of colonial relations of power in Australia, contributing to the health gap, however, did not accompany the referendum and to date has still not materialized (see, for example, Cunneen 2006).

In intimate femicide it is particularly important that women's deaths are counted in ways that allow recognition of the value of their lives and practically and symbolically demonstrate women's human rights, because women's progress towards the full range of human rights has been slow and patchy globally. It was not until the twentieth century, and after a fierce campaign by suffragettes and others in many different countries, that women won the right to vote in Western countries (Holton 1996). Until the mid- to late nineteenth century, women were likely to be formally and legally considered the property of their husbands (or fathers) and were unable to own property in their own right in many legal systems (Scutt 1990: 205). A husband was considered 'the lawful ruler' of the domestic unit so that a 'man's' home was considered his castle, in which he could treat 'his' wife and children as he wished (Scutt 1990: 446). Although the contemporary norm in Western countries is formal, legal equality between men and women, attitudes, and behaviours persist that continue to treat women as if they are objects rather than rights-bearing subjects (see, for example, Jordan 2018). Indeed, men's sense of sexual propriety over women has been found to be a common factor in intimate femicides (Polk 1994; see also Chapter 5). In the male-centric criminal justice system, this has translated in some countries into favourable legal outcomes for men who kill wives who were threatening to leave them or who had been unfaithful (on the operation of the provocation defence in excusing men's lethal violence, see Fitz-Gibbon 2014). Such policies and practices imply that some lives and some deaths matter more than others.

Whose deaths matter?

The importance of counting violent and/or avoidable deaths, particularly of minority, marginalized, and/or vilified groups, can be discerned in a range of political actions designed to resist the type of power-knowledge – deaths that do not count – that are produced as a result of deaths not counted. Here again the different meanings of 'counting' assist in highlighting the social stratification often expressed through the counting or not counting, accounting for or not accounting for, particular deaths/killings. The subtitle of the Geneva Declaration Secretariat's report on armed violence 'Every Body Counts' (2015) captures the focus on the counting of a wide range of types of deaths as a way of highlighting the value it places on *all* human life. From collecting quantitative data on deaths of irregular migrants attempting to cross national borders (Weber and Pickering 2011), Australian Aboriginal deaths in custody (Cunneen 2016), African American people shot and killed by police as part of the 'Black Lives Matter' movement (Lowery 2017), and the number of violent civilian deaths since the 2003 United States-led invasion of Iraq (Iraq Body Count 2018), counting violent deaths has been seen as a way of accounting for the deaths of people whose deaths are not officially counted. These 'herculean' attempts at data collection on lethality (Lowery 2017: 111–113 on 'Black Lives Matter') have often been led and undertaken by journalists, activists, and/or civil society groups. All of these counts have been mobilized to empower people to join together to challenge impunity and to encourage or force governments and powerful state actors to work to prevent these deaths by addressing the underlying issues that cause them. However, a note of caution is warranted at this point.

The justice aspirations of those undertaking these counts have not prevented those efforts from being co-opted by powerful actors in ways that maintain the marginalized or vilified status of the victims. Australian criminologists Weber and Pickering's (2011) quantification of deaths of irregular migrants attempting to cross national borders was aimed at highlighting the prevalence and costs of such deaths and the need for change. Their impulse was in line with their social justice and human rights aspirations and framing of irregular migrants, asylum seekers, and refugees. Primarily their work aimed to highlight the human costs of the securitization of borders against such groups and to encourage a more humanitarian policy response (Weber and Pickering 2011: 36). Subsequently Australian governments used the evidence about the number of border deaths, specifically the drowning deaths of those attempting to reach Australia by boat, to support a false humanitarianism completely at odds with the motivation behind Weber and Pickering's quantification. The government argued that punitive policies, such as the indefinite off-shore detention of those attempting to travel to Australia by boat in order to claim asylum, were a necessary deterrent aimed at saving the lives of potential asylum seekers who might otherwise attempt the journey to Australia (Pickering and Weber 2014). This example illustrates the ongoing politics of all counts and the need for active engagement with the why and what of such counts. It brings into sharp focus the risks of counting in terms of who has the power to make meaning of the resulting number(s) and how those meanings are then used.

The value of counting violence against women and intimate femicides

It is argued that data is central to ending violence generally and violence against women in particular. Careful attention to counting violence against women is seen as important in part because it is recognized as amongst the most underreported of crimes. It has only been in recent decades that violence against women, particularly by men they know, has been treated as real crime (see, for example, McCulloch 1985; Scutt 1990). Still, for many, there remains a widespread reluctance to report such crimes, and women who do report cannot rely on a sympathetic or even professional response (see, for example, Fitz-Gibbon et al. 2018).

The United Nations argues that data on violence against women can be used to

> enable informed decisions on where and how to target funding and other support ... Tracking data over time and monitoring trends can also support those designing and implementing programmes to more effectively evaluate the impact of their programmes. Among other uses, that data can then inform agencies' requests for additional funding. Proper use of VAWG [violence against women and girls] data can also empower survivors. By effectively presenting the issue as a national, sub-regional or even global preoccupation, women and girls will understand that they are not alone.
>
> (United Nations Population Fund 2013: 1)

So counting and measurement may help to understand the relative effectiveness of different approaches to responding to violence against women.

Walby and Towers (2017) point out that in order to prevent violence, a theory of change is necessary, which needs to link theory to empirical evidence. There are a number of theories that seek to explain violence against women and linked to these are a host of frequently overlapping approaches to preventing violence against women, including public health approaches, legal, behaviour change or psychological interventions, working with families, and addressing gender inequality. Each of these approaches posit different causal factors and different pathways to effective prevention (see McCulloch and Walklate forthcoming). Walby and Towers (2017: 12) highlight that systematic data is needed to 'test explanations, such as why rates of violence are higher or lower at different times, and in different locations, groups, policy regimes and social formations'. While they maintain surveys are the best way to discover the extent and distribution of violence, we argue here that counting homicides and intimate femicide is another way of counting and accounting for violence generally, and violence against women in particular. Crime statistics have a number of recognized limitations: many crimes are not reported to police or if reported are not recorded or do not proceed through the formal channels of the criminal justice system – investigation, prosecution, and conviction. This is less true of homicide, one of the most visible crimes, because it is considered the most serious of crimes (Brookman 2005: 2) and its consequences are generally evident. Still social divisions, particularly along 'race', class, and gender lines, impact significantly on what crimes are recorded and who is criminalized. Groups that are marginalized or excluded in social hierarchies are typically underrecognized as victims even when they are victims of femicide. The Canadian Femicide Observatory for Justice and Accountability records that:

> some femicides have not yet been reported or discovered, including those that may involve women and girls who have disappeared. This fact is most clearly demonstrated by the number of missing or disappeared Indigenous women and girls.
>
> (Dawson 2018: 4; see also National Inquiry
> MMIWG 2017; NWAC 2010)

When women and girls started to 'disappear' in large numbers in the Mexican town of Juarez in the early 1990s, such was the corruption and indifference of police and officials that the murders were not typically investigated and mothers' and women's groups had to organize to recover the bodies themselves from where they had been left across the countryside (Leal 2008). Similar patterns of indifference, corruption, and lack of effective investigation of femicides have been documented in the Northern Triangle of Central America (comprising El Salvador, Guatemala, and Honduras; see further Lozier 2018). Research in high-income countries likewise indicates that official intimate femicide counts are likely to be underestimates. Studies have found that murder scene staging aimed at concealing the criminal nature of a death is particularly prevalent in the case of intimate femicide (Hazelwood and Napier 2004; Keppel and Weis 2004) and that some deaths may be inaccurately recorded as natural deaths, accidents, or suicide. Vatnar et al. (2019) observe that many homicide-suicides are not fully investigated, yet their investigation of gendered patterns in Norway where men predominate as killers who then suicide resembles patterns of intimate partner homicide more closely than any other types of homicide. The gendered motives, however, are not recorded. In all of these instances, homicides statistics may offer considerably less than a full account of gendered killings.

Still homicide statistics are typically of higher quality than other crime statistics. The criteria for quality in relation to statistics generally include characteristics such as relevance, accuracy and reliability, timeliness and punctuality, accessibility and clarity, and coherence and comparability (see, for example, Office of National Statistics UK 2013: 7). An Australian project aimed at developing a 'family violence index' considered that the criteria for quality data to be included were transparency, reliability and consistency, comparability, accessibility, and sensitivity to change. They determined that homicide data met these criteria, with the exception of the last, and found a lag of three or four years in the availability of homicide data (Ross et al. 2017: 47). However, not all homicides are femicides and not all femicides are intimate femicides, so, apart from the time lag in the accessibility of data, there are other issues that need to be considered in relation to the quality of data currently in existence and that might be collected in the future. One advantage of focusing on intimate femicide is that the definition of these femicides is relatively straightforward – an intimate femicide occurs where the female victim and the male perpetrator are current or former partners, whether married, de facto married, or boy/girlfriend. It is the case, however, that differences remain in the definition of relationship, there are different approaches to including attempted homicides, and different criminal codes combine to give rise to challenges in comparability between jurisdictions where data is collected. Despite this, the *relative* simplicity of the definition of intimate femicide means that the comparability of data across jurisdictions is potentially high. However, as Walby and Towers (2017: 13) maintain, there are at least four dimensions needed in order to capture the gendered nature of violence: the victim's sex, the perpetrator's sex, the relationship between perpetrator and victim, and whether there is a sexual motive for the killing. The first three data points are essential to the classification of intimate femicides. Overcoming the lack of data in many jurisdictions about the relationship between the perpetrator and victim will be critical moving forward if systematic, quality data is to be collected on intimate femicides worldwide and if any progress towards prevention in whatever shape or form it takes is to be made.

Conclusion

It is important not to underestimate the difficulties of preventing intimate femicide and the many challenges that exist in term of understanding and implementing risk frameworks that attempt to predict and/or prevent fatal outcomes. However, without reliable information about prevalence, trends over time and between locations, there is no way to track the effectiveness of policy interventions and to allocate resources in ways that are best targeted at effective intervention and ultimately the prevention of these killings. A better system of intimate femicide data collection and reporting might

> contribute to increased public awareness and demand for a public health sector response … as well as providing concrete information on risk factors and risk groups to guide police, legal, educational, and political forces in development of prevention strategies and services.
>
> (Vives-Cases et al. 2016: 14)

Moreover, the weight of numbers associated with counting intimate femicide might also contribute to understanding such violence as a manifestation of the continuing gender inequality and the different vectors of power and control that drive such violence. The weight assigned to numbers in testing and/or supporting conceptual understandings of such violence validates the importance of counting as one way of ensuring women's lives count.

References

Academic Council on the United Nations System. (2017). *Femicide VII: Establishing a Femicide Watch in Every Country.* Vienna: ACUNS. Available at: https://acuns.org/femicide-volume-vii-establishing-a-femicide-watch-in-every-country/

Bayatrizi, Z. (2009). Counting the dead and regulating the living: early modern statistics and the formation of the sociological imagination (1662–1897) *British Journal of Sociology*, 60(3): 603–621.

Bugeja, L., Butler, A., Buxton, E., Ehrat, H., Hayes, M., McIntyre, S.-J. and Walsh, C. (2013). The implementation of domestic violence death reviews in Australia. *Homicide Studies* 17: 353.

Booth, J.W. (2001). The unforgotten: memories of justice. *American Political Science Review*, 95(4): 777–791.

Brookman, F. (2005). *Understanding Homicide*. London, Thousand Oaks, New Delhi: Sage Publications.

Crenshaw, K. (1989). Demarginalizing the intersection of race and sex: a black feminist critique of antidiscrimination doctrine, feminist theory and antiracist politics, U. Chi. Legal F. 139.

Cullen, P., Vaughan, G., Zhuoyang, L., Price, J., Yu, D., and Sullivan, E. (2018). Counting dead women in Australia: An in-depth case review of femicide. *Journal of Family Violence*, 34(1): 1–8.

Cunneen, C. (2006). Aboriginal deaths in custody: a continuing systematic abuse. *Social Justice* 33(4) (106), Deaths in Custody and Detention, 37–51.

Dawson, M. (2018). The Canadian femicide observatory for justice and accountability report. Available at: https://femicideincanada.ca

Dearden, W. and Jones, W. (2008). Homicide in Australia: 2006-2007 National Homicide Monitoring Program Annual Report, Australian Institute of Criminology, Canberra.

Dekeseredy, W., Burnham, K., Nicewarner, R., Nolan, J., and Hall-Sanchez, A., (forthcoming) Aggrieved entitlement in the ivory tower: exploratory qualitative results from a large-scale campus climate survey. *Journal of Qualitative Criminal Justice and Criminology*.

Department of Prime Minister and Cabinet (2019). Closing the gap report, Australian Government. Available at: https://ctgreport.niaa.gov.au

Fitz-Gibbon, K. (2014). *Homicide Law Reform, Gender and the Provocation Defence: A Comparative Perspective*. Palgrave MacMillan: New Hampshire.

Fitz-Gibbon, K., Walklate, S., McCulloch, J. and Maher, J. (2018). Introduction: Intimate partner violence, risk and security- securing women's lives in a global world. In K. Fitz-Gibbon, S. Walklate, J. McCulloch, and J. Maher (eds) *Intimate Partner Violence, Risk and Security-Securing Women's Lives in a Global World*, pp. 1–16. London and New York: Routledge.

Foucault, M. (1977). *Discipline and Punish: The Birth of the Prison*. Harmondsworth: Penguin.

Gardiner-Garden, J. (2007). The 1967 Referendum—history and myths Parliamentary Research Brief, Parliament of Australia, Department of Parliamentary Services. Available at: https://parlinfo.aph.gov.au/parlInfo/download/library/prspub/JTZM6/upload_binary/jtzm62.pdf

Geneva Declaration Secretariat. (2015). *Global Burden of Armed Violence 2015: Every Body Counts* (Global Burden of Armed Violence). Cambridge: Cambridge University Press. doi:10.1017/CBO9781107707108

58 *Why counting matters*

Hazelwood, R.R. and Napier, M.R. (2004). Crime scene staging and its detection. *International Journal of Offender Therapy and Comparative Criminology*, 48(6): 744–759.
Hoeffler, A. and Fearon, J. (2015). *Post-2015 Consensus: Conflict and Violence Assessment*. Copenhagen: Copenhagen Consensus Center.
Holton, S. (1996). *Suffrage Days: Stories from the Women's Suffrage Movement*. London and New York: Routledge.
Iraq Body Count. (2018). Available at: www.iraqbodycount.org
Jordan, J. (2018). Surveying the womanscape: objectification, self-objectification and intimate partner violence. In K. Fitz-Gibbon, S. Walklate, J. McCulloch, and J.M. Maher (eds) *Intimate Partner Violence Risk and Security: Securing Women's Lives in a Global World*, pp. 88–106. Oxon and New York: Routledge.
Keppel, R.D. and Weis, J.G. (2004). The rarity of 'unusual' dispositions of victim bodies: staging and posing. *Journal of Forensic Science*, 49(6): 1308–1312.
Leal, L. (2008). 'Combating impunity and femicide in Ciudad Juarez' NACL Report on the Americas, 41(3): 31–40.
Lozier, L. (2018). Mapping gender violence narratives in the Northern Triangle of Central America. In K. Fitz-Gibbon, S. Walklate, J. McCulloch, and J.M. Maher (eds) *Intimate Partner Violence, Risk and Security: Securing Women's Lives in a Global World*, pp. 109–125. London and New York: Routledge.
Lowery, W. (2017). *"They Can't Kill Us All": The Story of Back Lives Matter*. London: Penguin Books.
McCulloch, J. (1985). Police response to domestic violence, Victoria. In S.E. Hatty (ed) *Domestic Violence*, pp. 523–530. Canberra: Australian Institute of Criminology.
McCulloch, J. and Walklate, S. (forthcoming). Rendering the ordinary extra-ordinary in order to facilitate prevention: the case of (sexual) violence against women. In C. Barlow and S. Kewley (eds) *Preventing Sexual Violence*. Bristol: Policy Press.
Merry, S.E. (2016). *The Seductions of Quantification: Measuring Human Rights, Gender Violence, and Sex Trafficking*. Chicago, IL: University of Chicago Press.
National Inquiry into Missing and Murdered Indigenous Women and Girls. (2017). Our women and girls are sacred: interim report. Ottawa: National Inquiry.
Native Women's Association of Canada (NWAC). (2010). *What Their Stories Tell Us: Research Findings from the Sisters in Spirit Initiative*. Ottawa: NWAC.
Office for National Statistics. (2013). *Guidelines on Measuring Statistical Output Quality. V4.1*. Newport: Office of National Statistics.
Pickering, S. and Weber, L. (2014). New deterrence scripts in Australia's rejuvenated offshore detention regime for asylum seekers. *Law & Social Inquiry*, 39(4): 1006–1026.

Polk, K. (1994). *When Men Kill: Scenario of Masculine Violence.* Cambridge: Cambridge University Press.

Ross, S., Hegarty, K., Forsdike, K., and Diemer, K. (2017). Family Violence Index, Submitted by to the Department of Premier and Cabinet by Melbourne University on behalf of Australia's National Research Organisation for Women's Safety.

Scutt, J. (1990). *Women and the Law: Commentary and Materials.* Perth, WA: Law Book Company.

United Nations Population Fund (2013) The role of data in addressing violence against women and girls. Available at: www.unfpa.org/sites/default/files/resource-pdf/finalUNFPA_CSW_Book_20130221_Data.pdf

Vatnar, S.K.B., Friestad, C., and Bjørkly, S. (2019). A comparison of intimate partner homicide with intimate partner homicide-suicide: evidence from a Norwegian national 22-year cohort. *Journal of Interpersonal Violence.* doi:10.1177/0886260519849656

Virueda, M. and Payne, J. (2010). Homicide in Australia: 2007–08 National Homicide Monitoring Program Annual Report, Monitoring Reports No. 13, Australian Institute of Criminology, Canberra. Available at: https://aic.gov.au/publications/mr/mr13

Vives-Cases, C., Goicolea, I., Hernández, A., Sanz-Barbero, B., Gill, A.K., Baldry, A.C., et al. (2016). Expert opinions on improving femicide data collection across Europe: a concept mapping study. *PLoS ONE,* 11(2): e0148364. doi:10.1371/journal. pone.0148364

Walby, S. and Towers, J. (2017). Measuring violence to end violence: mainstreaming gender. *Journal of Gender-Based Violence,* 1(1): 11–31, doi: 10.1332/239868017X14913081639155

Watts, C. and Zimmerman, C. (2002). Violence against women: global scope and magnitude. *The Lancet,* 359(9313): 1232–1237.

Weber, L. and Pickering, S. (2011). *Globalization and Borders: Death at the Global Frontier.* Basingstoke: Palgrave Macmillan.

Webster, K. (2016). A preventable burden: measuring and addressing the prevalence and health impacts of intimate partner violence in Australian women (ANROWS Compass, 07/2016), Sydney: ANROWS.

Weil, S. and Kouta, C. (2017). Femicide a glance through qualitative lenses. *Qualitative Sociology Review,* 13(3): 6–13.

World Health Organisation. (2013). Global and regional estimates of violence against women: prevalence and health effects of intimate partner violence and non-partner sexual violence. Switzerland. Available at www.who.int/reproductivehealth/publications/violence/9789241564625/en/

4 The risks of counting the killing of women

Introduction

In the previous chapters, we argued for the value of counting and the advocacy work that has been done to create counts in order to capture the global patterns of systematic violence against women. This has particular salience in the emerging counts of intimate femicides as the most extreme evidence of violence against women. In this chapter, we examine more fully the limitations and problems of counting. In our view there are a number of key critical risks in feminist political projects of counting intimate femicide. The first concerns what we know about the data limitations in existing counts in terms of who is counted and who is not counted and what knowledge about intimate femicides and risks this incomplete data then creates. The second key risk pertains to what it is that underpins our conceptualizations and practices of counting. Creating counts, indexes, or any form of quantifiable measures about the meaning and value of human lives relies on the development of a series of shared questions and assumptions, and as we know, embedding gender into such analyses has never been and is still not a straightforward process. This leads to the third critical risk we have identified – the relationship between the counts of intimate femicide and theories of gender change and prevention, neither of which have yet been fully articulated or understood. Consequently, as Bradshaw and Norman (2013) observe, data on trends and patterns that reveal how gender is working in these homicides is still limited. This means there are gaps and confusions in both our existing counts and our understandings of what these counts might mean. If we are to mobilize counts of intimate femicide to inform prevention efforts, we need the ability to predict and the ability to intervene (McCulloch and Walklate forthcoming); both of these proactive actions require a grounded and clear understanding of what different counts mean and how outcomes can be changed. Counts alone cannot provide enough information or knowledge to achieve everyday security for women, their safety from the lethal violence inflicted by male partners, nor can they illuminate the broader social structures that drive such violence. One view is, as Dawson (2018a) observed, that the prevention of intimate femicide requires an 'ecological' approach to risks and change, one which encompasses individual, social, and structural levels. However, it is difficult to envisage change at any of these levels without a reliable understanding of the nature and extent of the problem being addressed. At the same time, counting the killings of women by their intimate partners may offer a critical platform towards change and prevention of intimate femicide, but it will never be sufficient. The gravity and extent of men's lethal violence against women underlines the need for efforts at multiple levels and from varied perspectives.

The critical work of counting the gendered killing of women requires effective processes of quantification. Revealing the numbers and patterns of such killings requires attention to the gendered social structures and institutions underpinning and enabling these killings, and this requires critical acuity in relation to the data collected and what this data means. Thapar-Björkert et al. (2016) use the term 'symbolic violence' to illuminate the elements that work to oppress women and the need for the appreciation of these elements to be built into any effective and comprehensive gendered analysis. They describe the elementary modes of domination, such as direct physical violence, but also recognize there are complementary modes of domination enforcing gendered inequalities and the gendered violence(s) surrounding them. Structural complicity and institutional silencing (Thapar-Björkert et al. 2016) support the commission of everyday violence and intimate femicide as violence against women as well as through processes that render invisible and/or impede social and individual accountability for such crimes. As we turn to measuring numbers of killings, including and understanding the effects, impacts, and outcomes of social stratifications grounded in sexism, racism, ableism, and misogyny, it is taken as given that these influence the production of numbers, the ways in which they are produced, and operate as complementary modes of domination. These processes are fraught and difficult but are critically important in order to understand who and what is being counted. Given that one of the objectives of counting is to provide incontrovertible evidence about the phenomenon under investigation, there is a risk that if the evidence base cannot effectively integrate and make visible the results produced by these intersecting oppressions, such counts may generate and/or further embed structural and symbolic violence(s). In what follows we identify the ways in which these kinds of risk can manifest themselves.

The first risk: the data gaps and their consequences

There is considerable consensus that existing global counts of intimate femicides, of the killings of women, and of homicides are all limited by missing data (Stöckl et al. 2013). Stöckl et al. (2013) observe that in many official or police-based counts, a key limitation in identifying prevalence of intimate femicide is the failure to record the relationship between the victim and the offender. As Walby and Towers (2017) have argued, information on this relationship is fundamental to understanding the meaning and impact of sex and gender in the count. Even where national organizations have adopted the term 'femicide' and collect data under this rubric, the definition varies from country to country, meaning the data will not be readily comparable (UNDOC 2018). As the Global Homicide Report (UNDOC 2018) contends, developing counts inevitably requires the use of proxies to identify gender-related deaths and then to assign them to a relevant category of femicide.

Building a count of intimate femicides utilizing proxies (that is, assuming equivalence between definitions where none may exist) introduces considerable risks of misinterpretation of national and local data, which in turn may potentially confuse and obscure the operation of gender impacts such as inequality. Definitions of femicide may need augmentation to capture the gendered social processes that lead to women's murders at the hands of their intimates and in some instances to deaths not readily identified as killings but that are nevertheless the outcome of gendered violence. Shalhoub-Kevorkian (2003) examines femicides in Palestine and argues the threats of murder that subtend the everyday lives of these women mean they live effectively on death row – and their lives and deaths must thus be understood within this continuum. It is recognized that most women in prison have direct experiences of partner violence and similarly that they die at disproportionate rates in terms of their ages and sex (Carlton and Segrave 2011); yet these untimely deaths are not linked to intimate partner violence (see also Sherman and Harris 2015). In particular, even when the intimate partner is clearly the perpetrator, the killings of those who have been systematically marginalized or made invisible are much less likely to be captured accurately inside these flawed datasets. The invisibility of femicide deaths where there is no physical body is also an issue requiring further contemplation and excavation (Ferguson and Pooley 2019).

As discussed earlier in this volume, there are numerous identified instances where the killings of particular groups of women have not been counted or seen as femicides, such as in Ciudad Juárez and for indigenous women and girls in Canada (Corradi et al. 2016; Dawson 2018b; National Inquiry into Missing and Murdered Indigenous Women and Girls 2019). True (2015) has observed that these gaps in recording are not incidental; rather, the social and cultural preconditions that hide intimate femicides, and femicides more broadly, along with other forms of gendered violence, are the same preconditions that create them. 'In other words, the causes of (historical and continued) underreporting are linked to the causes of sexual and gender-based violence (SGBV)' (True 2015: 561).

These lacunae emphasize why a critical approach to existing data, the terminology, and presuppositions we use to create counts, what it is we expect counts to show, and how we link this process to prevention and social change require consistent critical attention and re-evaluation. In fact, we argue that this need to qualify, augment, and consistently recreate definitions of femicides, and intimate femicides following Stout (1992), who coined the term, is central to the counts that can be built if we are to take gender seriously. We need also to look beyond the concept of missing data narrowly configured to the broader risk inherent in all forms of counting. Corradi et al. (2016), in their review of the diverse uses of femicide and the complexity of definitional clarity, capture this broader risk:

> A second weakness is operational. How can we capture the misogynist motivation, the assumption that this particular woman was murdered, 'simply because she is a woman'?
>
> (Corradi et al. 2016: 980)

How do we count effectively and accurately when part of what it is we are seeking to count is embedded attitudinal and systemic prejudice towards and hatred of women that cannot be readily measured? How do we measure the patriarchal constructions that Shalhoub-Kevorkian (2003) argues actually sustain existing social structures, meaning lethality is in fact a necessary and expected outcome of some women's lives rather than an anomaly? In such an instance, the concept of risk is turned on its head.

In our view, the dilemma identified here creates additional and significant risks in counting that compound the already serious ones born of error, invisibility, and marginalization. These additional risks are linked to the epistemological dissonance between the aims and objectives of quantification more generally and the effective and meaningful embedding of gender in the counts of killings of women and intimate femicides in particular. The expectations of prevention and increased social justice we assume or hope will emerge from knowledge of the 'how many' femicides are central to calls for global indexes and responses. Yet without shared articulations of how and what we are counting, we risk producing decontextualized numbers that mark only individual incidents rather than the more complex work of recognizing and remembering those women who have been killed by their male intimate partners. It is the risk of a 'thin' set of numbers, rather than a memorial that records and remembers each killing, which threatens these goals rather than a thick and ecologically effective database to sustain and support prevention and ultimately women's everyday security. There is also the risk that the focus on individual men and the violence directly linked to the killing of women will elide the broader structural factors that create a fertile context for such killings.

Such a focus also fails to recognize that violence against women, and intimate partner violence in particular, leads to an incalculable number of women's untimely deaths. It is well documented that intimate partner violence (IPV) is linked to negative health outcomes and disability, substance abuse, poverty, and homelessness, all of which are likely to lead to result in early death (Franzway 2015; Webster 2016). Intimate femicide counts may capture violent deaths, but they cannot capture the full extent of men's lethal violence, if we understand that term to capture early deaths caused by such violence. They reveal little, in how they are currently conceptualized, about slow femicide.

The second risk: counting as both a practice and an epistemological framework

The development of social science research methods (and particularly the emphasis on the importance on quantification and counting in the social sciences), as Ann Oakley (2000) has argued, reflected a political engagement with the dominance of science itself and with scientific method as the best and most reliable form of generating knowledge. The differential value within and external to the social sciences attributed to quantitative and qualitative social science inquiry, she argues, can be seen as an outcome of ongoing contests about who knows best and how they know. These scales of value create the cadre of 'experts' and sets of evidence that governments, policy makers, international bodies, and other civil society organizations place most confidence in, referred to by Merry (2016) as expertise inertia These same scales simultaneously marginalize other forms of knowledge and information. For Oakley (2000), ways of knowing can only ever be understood in the context of how they arose and the foundational nature of gender, or its absence, found in all epistemologies and the empirical outcomes they produce:

> Thus, neither methods, nor methodology can be understood except in the context of gendered social relations. Understanding this involves a mapping of how gender, women, nature and knowledge have been constructed both inside and outside all forms of science.
>
> (Oakley 2000: 4)

When we assess the risks of counting the killing of women then, it is critically important we recognize the processes of acquiring knowledge by counting as well as all the specific risks embedded in counting intimate femicide such as data gaps, invisibilities, how such collated knowledges might be used, and how these are already embedded in gendered political projects of knowledge production. We know 'the availability of quantitative data is changing the nature of politics and public policy locally and globally' (Ackerly and True 2018: 271), but the tenor and nature of such change requires ongoing attention and pressure for accountability. Critical attention must be directed not only at who knows and how they know but also and always to the limitations of what they can know.

The move to capture and to work towards quantification of the killing of women, especially at the hands of their intimate partners, and the relationships and patterns of gendered violence(s) that precede such deaths, binds accounts of gender-based violence to existing norms and structures. As Ackerly and True (2018: 263) have observed, 'all research questions are ultimately normative, reflecting a particular historical time, space and subjectivity'. The use of the terms 'killings' or more specifically 'intimate femicides' and 'women' in such an equation may lead to presuppositions that the term 'women' is sufficient to make visible the killings that we aim to count and need to count. But Walby and Towers (2017) have argued that sex, as exemplified in the term 'women' is not sufficient to embed gender effectively in measurement. Ackerly and True (2018) similarly observe that sex-based violence does not fully equate to gender-based violence, with its broader capture of the impacts of gendered violence that are not yet seen. These distinctions are important because they illuminate the risks and gaps that can emerge in progress towards a shared global index of intimate femicides.

The creation of the term 'femicide' and its variations globally (such as 'feminicide' in South American countries, see further Pierobom de Avila 2018) is a form of interrogation of what is known and assumed about patterns of death and killings (Ackerly and True 2018). Corradi et al. (2016) trace the explicit political project in the development of femicide research and studies. Yet this effort to distinguish homicides where women die because they are women is a development and divergence from the generalized drive in social sciences to better identify patterns of lethal killings in order to prevent and minimize them (Bayatrizi 2009). This effort has animated social science inquiries from their inception and plays a key part in the critical contribution of social sciences to social progress through the development of accurate knowledge about patterns of violent death. As Bayatrizi (2009: 609) explains:

> Writing in the shadows of death and destruction caused by civil wars, Hobbes' work (1978 [1651]; 1983 [1642]) was premised on the assumption that the passage from the natural state of war of all against all to a peaceful state of civil society is primarily predicated on a given society's moral and political attitude toward life and death and, in particular, its ability to minimize the use, presence, and potential threat of violent death.

Bayatrizi (2009) has observed that the development of statistical knowledges in particular formed a critical part of how societies began to think about and understand risk particularly as it pertained to violent deaths that occurred out of time: 'Eighteenth century statisticians reconceptualized life, not as a divine destiny or a personal fate but as a process amenable to risk calculation and management' (Bayatrizi 2009: 613). However, as the emergence of femicide in the early 1990s signals, these statistical patterns and studies were not accounting for or recognizing gender.

The movement to develop comprehensive and accurate data that fully embeds gender and allows for the counting of gendered violence and all different types of gendered homicides has been much slower and did not automatically emerge from the trend towards risk assessment and management around violent deaths. For the gendering of fatal risks to become visible required the reconfiguration of ideas about data, data collection, measurement, and what measurement is for. It requires acknowledgement, following Shalhoub-Kevorkian (2003), that the language of risk may not be adequate to achieve prevention where accepted social and political structures of profound and systemic gender inequality exist. Such structures contribute to and in fact underpin patterns of intimate femicide, so prevention – requiring both identification and intervention (McCulloch and Walklate forthcoming) – is potentially unachievable. This acknowledgement means that we recognize intimate femicides as likely outcomes of everyday gendered patterns rather than as risks of deviation or system failures. In this context, ecological change (Dawson 2018b) is not achieved in the social project of quantification that Bayatrizi (2009) described, as the existing social structures even when operating optimally, including its processes of inquiry and quantification, are the source of the problem rather than any part of the solution.

It is clearly the work of feminist activism, remembering, and research to change the ways we understand what it is that we see and know. 'The tools of feminism make the invisible visible and the familiar strange, and can open up the gendered nature of politics and the politics of gender relations' (Ackerly and True 2006: 260, 2018). Feminist interventions into practices of counting femicide, or making gender count in how we understand women's deaths at the hands of men, have had to, in the first instance, create the methodological and conceptual tools to build new empirical datasets showing gender patterns and homicide prevalence. This work has been critical in building towards the global consensus that the killing of women and girls is gender-related (UNDOC 2018). Feminist work has made and continues to make critical 'contribution to the methodology for collecting the data needed to develop and test a theory of change for gendered violence' (Walby and Towers 2017:12).

However, in line with the decades of activism, scholarship, and contest to have domestic violence recognized as a crime, rather than a private matter, the development of nuanced gendered homicide data that illuminates such patterns and the ensuing contributions to prevention are still not in place. While 'feminist scholars analyze private sphere domestic violence as both a form of political violence (Cockburn 2010) and a precondition for more visible violence against women in the public sphere' (True 2015: 555), there has been considerable reluctance to embed this dynamic nexus in many national and global approaches. Walby et al. (2015) offer a critical example of this reluctance or absence in their argument that recent discussions in Western criminology about the reduction in incidences of violence have generally failed to systematically include gender analysis despite the fact that patterns revealed by such analyses clearly include gendered trends. In addition Caman et al. (2017) offer a valuable illustration of this absence in their discussion of changing patterns of intimate partner homicide in Canada. As they observe, there has been a decrease in the numbers of male partner victims in comparison to female partner victims in recent decades. They point to women's increased financial autonomy, the growth in protective services, and changes in approaches to domestic violence as perhaps supporting women to leave abusive relationships, thereby reducing fatal outcomes for men. They suggest the unchanging nature of the male-perpetrated killings of their female partners may be attributed to 'backlash', in response to men's perceived loss of control. However, such explanations necessarily remain theoretical in nature as the longitudinal and nuanced data collection and analysis to reveal and understand such patterns do not yet exist.

Beyond these layers of risk, however, there is another deeper layer that is also a critical risk in projects of counting. When we focus our attention and activism on counting the killing of women, we then become part of these knowledge projects that have so successfully maintained the invisibility of gendered violence(s) of all types. If there is widespread recognition that data collected on gender violence in all its forms is poor (Ackerly and True 2018; True 2015; Walby and Towers 2017; Walby et al. 2015) and that work on prevalence of intimate femicides is still patchy and incomplete (Corradi et al. 2016; Stockl et al. 2013) and we continue to focus our attention there, we run the risk of continuing to exclude or marginalize other critical forms of knowledge about these deaths. True (2015) and Walby et al. (2015) outline the persistence of data-gathering patterns that do not actually work with gender but rather use 'sex' simply defined as a proxy. Such approaches are very unlikely to capture the work of gender in these killings, as they do not even capture the work of gender in the counting. In emphasizing the importance of counts, in our adherence to and reification of this methodology for understanding gender-based violence and homicides, we may not be able to maintain enough critical distance from the epistemological settings that made women and gender invisible in the first place. Corradi et al. (2016) have suggested there has been a loss of political 'thrust' as femicide has been woven into a broad range of measures, indicators, and indices. While Merry (2016) clearly demonstrates that all forms of counting and measuring are political and that successful measures are always a product of 'cultural work', these processes tend to be hidden in the publication and dissemination of the measures. Conventional uses of numbers tend to simplify and decontextualize. They may distort what is to be known. Those who define the indicators and indexes have the opportunity to create and divide forms of truth (Merry 2016) and also the opportunity to exclude other truths.

The third risk: commissioning or facilitating structural violence(s)

Merry (2016) argues that the turn to evidence-based governance seeks 'soft change'; such technologies of governance she suggests are focused on results-based policy development. Yet, for us this does raise a question about what the 'results' might be of an intensive focus on counting intimate femicides and seeking to build our prevention strategies for change on this approach. As we have been arguing throughout this chapter and book, any time we identify, gather, and collect data on any form of gendered violence we will be influenced by, and part of creating knowledge and social processes that are always already gendered and oppressive: all societies, cultures, communities, and everyday interactions are threaded with gender inequality. Such inequalities rely on and reinforce the structural complicity and institutional silencing (Thapar-Björkert et al. 2016), supporting the commission of everyday violence and intimate femicide and making counting so difficult.

These risks are illuminated in a number of different ways. For example, Nicole Rafter's (2016) exploration of genocide identifies the relative absence of gendered analysis in genocide literature despite the presence of sex and sexual violence in counts and analyses. Her examination of the operation of gender in the Rwandan genocide reveals the importance of pre-existing inequalities, misogyny, and expectations of unpaid care labour, all gendered norms, in patterns of perpetration and victimization. Rafter charts a necessary movement from the analysis of women's social roles: what women did and how they were affected, towards the analysis of the operation of gender; the role of masculinity in the commission of genocide; and how norms of femininity impacted women's experiences of violence and responsibilities assigned to those who acted. Without mobilizing this gendered analysis, the data we gather and our consequent understandings of violence(s) and killings and their meanings and impacts will be critically inadequate.

In responses to domestic and family violence and intimate femicide, these gendered patterns are at the centre of both the crimes committed and to the development of effective responses. The 'truths' we may not see when we count the killing of women by male partners for the most part include those who have committed the crimes. In focusing our attention on counting women killed by their male intimate partner, we need to move towards the creation of counts that make those who have perpetrated such homicides accountable and fully visible too.

When we gather and collate data on those who have died as a result of intimate femicides, there is a risk that we make these women the focus of investigation and interrogation in ways that may reinforce the long-standing tendency of the justice systems and social discourses to blame the women as in some way responsible for their violent deaths.

The challenge is to bring the woman who has been killed into focus in a way that acknowledges her life and properly memorializes it. A key change in how we think about accountability for family violence has been the insistence that the responsibility lies with the perpetrator. When we count, we need to ensure we are not unwittingly maintaining a focus on those who are victims. In all forms of family violence, the data gathered on those who have experienced such violence or been victims of it is much more in view of the system than data or information on those who have perpetrated it. Walby et al's (2015) account of the capping of serious crimes in most victimization surveys is a clear example of this gap: a direct impact is the capping of personal crimes by a third. Thus data on crimes of domestic or intimate partner violence is reduced: men's repeated violence against women is rendered at least partially invisible.

In contrast, assessments of women's characters as victims of fatal violence, as deficient mothers, as responsible for men's violence and rage abound in national legal systems, and waves of reform have not been able to eradicate the gendered underpinnings in all forms of national and international instruments that regulate security, justice, and responsibility. If we only count women, we will not be able to see and stop the gendered violence that men commit. As Merry (2016: 12) says, 'the process of measurement tends to produce the phenomenon it claims to measure'. If we are to take gender seriously, our measurements need to be focused on perpetration and individual responsibility as well as visibility and accuracy.

Conclusion

The process of recognizing intimate partner violence as violence has required sustained advocacy, argumentation, and contest. To recognize intimate violence as a serious harm, to attend to the associated and/or consequent measurements of such violence(s), and to accept this violence as a public responsibility rather than a private harm have taken many decades of feminist activist and scholarly work. This ongoing, slow but significant process of change has required the development of a new architecture of gendered knowledges: epistemology, methodologies, and analytic approaches that have allowed us to begin to see the violence and in turn the deaths of women at the hands of male intimate partners and what it means.

This counting work has and continues to be important, but it is also risky. In measuring intimate femicides, there is consensus that the data that exists is not comprehensive or accurate (Stockl et al. 2013), and it is clear that this lack of data quality will impact what can be known about intimate femicides. It is also clear that the commitment to counting femicide does not necessarily equate to a commitment to embed gender critically and effectively in such counts. This 'thin' or limited commitment to gender analysis, which tends to use sex as a proxy, will have an effect on how we understand and theorize links between what we 'know' from the collected data and numbers and what this means in terms of social patterns and most importantly in terms of outcomes. Measuring patriarchy as it undergirds all forms of violence against women is still a complex, and in some contexts an unpalatable, task.

Internationally in attending to gendered violence and all forms of family violence, there is increasing recognition that prevention is critical to achieving a future free from violence. There is greater willingness to link broader indicators of gender (in)equality to patterns and prevalence of gendered violence and to work towards solutions aimed at changing these patterns. Yet the ways in which we might effectively link risk assessment around gendered and family violence and intimate femicides specifically to successful prevention, including effective interventions, are not yet clear. Risks are most often focused on individual accounting against a series of assessment criteria: counts of deaths also are focused on individual crimes, events, and numbers. The risk is that counting focuses us on fatalities and does not produce a clear framework for embedding social frameworks in that count. The risk is also that we do not see or fully count the commission of gendered violence(s) at the root of these killings. There is evidence that the serious risk of not counting the killings of women already marginalized is not simply a risk but is already limiting and corrupting existing counts. The National Inquiry into Missing and Murdered Indigenous Women and Girls in Canada, which finished its work this year, makes this clear: existing measures of homicides are not capturing the deaths of many women let alone providing information on the relevant gendered patterns in order to support prevention. In combination, the Inquiry suggests this is a race-based genocide.

Recognizing these risks of symbolic violence (Thapar-Björkert et al. 2016), in structural violence(s) and institutional silencing, allows us to think more critically about the work that numbers do, about their propensity to simplify what it is that we know and what we need to do about it. Statistics and process of quantification emerged as a critical activity for the building of states and the hierarchical regulation of lives within those states (Bayatrizi 2009). These measurements have only just started to make visible gendered patterns of violence and death. Although these were always about connecting individual incidents and outcomes to broader social patterns, for a very long time, this work systematically excluded gender. For Shalhoub-Kevorkian, this exclusion of gender is not an absence simply emerging from ignorance or invisibility. It is rather a necessary exclusion for the maintenance of our existing social worlds, as explained:

> This view of femicide derives from the central argument (which I believe should be at the heart of human rights and feminist debates) that sexism and gender oppression do not just refer to the binary relations between men and women, or the causal relations between patriarchy and female abuse, but constitute the central social dynamic of the world that recreates, maintains, and justifies a pervasive, inhumane social abuse.
>
> (Shalhoub-Kevorkian 2003: 582)

If we are to address the multiple and diverse risks that come from counting, and if we recognize, following Ackerly and True (2018), that all forms of research are inherently normative, the challenge may be to keep reflecting on the tools of social change that we are engaging with, changing our questions and our processes and approach to measurement to make sure what we are counting and the way we are counting are focused on what it is we want to change. We also need to recognize that counting alone is not enough: 'The importance of involving multiple sectors is premised on the view that violence is a multifaceted problem that cannot be addressed with a single-factor solution' (Canadian Femicide Observatory for Justice and Accountability 2019: np).

References

Ackerly, B. and True, J. (2018). With or without feminism? Researching gender and politics in the 21st century. *European Journal of Politics and Gender*, 1(1–2): 259–278.

Ackerly, B.A. and True, J. (2006). Studying the struggles and wishes of the age: feminist theoretical methodology and feminist theoretical methods. In B.A. Ackerly, M. Stern, and J. True (eds) *Feminist Methodologies for International Relations*, pp. 241–260. Cambridge: Cambridge University Press.

Bayatrizi, Z. (2009). Counting the dead and regulating the living: early modern statistics and the formation of the sociological imagination (1662–1897). *British Journal of Sociology*, 60(3): 603–621.

Bradshaw, R. and Norman, D. (2013). What is the scale of intimate partner homicide? *The Lancet*, 382. September 7. Available at: www.thelancet.com

Caman, S., Kristiansson, M., Granath, S., and Sturup, J. (2017). Trends in rates and characteristics of intimate partner homicides between 1990 and 2013. *Journal of Criminal Justice*, 49: 14–21.

Canadian Femicide Observatory for Justice and Accountability. (2019). Preventing femicide. Available at: www.femicideincanada.ca/preventing [Accessed 10 May 2019]

Carlton, B. and Segrave, M. (2011). Women's survival post-imprisonment: connecting imprisonment with pains past and present. *Punishment & Society*, 13(5): 551–570.

Cockburn, C. (2010). Gender relations as causal in militarization and war: A feminist standpoint. *International Feminist Journal of Politics*, 12(2): 139–157.

Corradi, C., Marcuello-Servós, C., Boira, S., and Weil, S. (2016). Theories of femicide and their significance for social research. *Current Sociology*, 64(7): 975–995.

Dawson, M. (2018a). Femicide in Canada: Accountability and punishment. *AC System, Femicide IX: Femicide, State Accountability and Punishment*, pp. 14–23. Available at: https://acuns.org/femicide-volume-ix-femicide-state-accountability-and-punishment/ [Accessed 12 June 2019]

Dawson, M. (2018b). The Canadian femicide observatory for justice and accountability report. Available at: https://femicideincanada.ca [Accessed 10 May 2019]

Ferguson, C. and Pooley, K. (2019). No-body intimate partner homicides in Australia: Exploring solved cases. Paper presented to the 3rd European Conference on Domestic Violence, Oslo, September.

Franzway, S., Wendt, S., Moulding, N., Zufferey, C., Chung, D., and Elder, A. (2015). Gender violence and citizenship: the long-term effects of domestic violence on mental health, housing, work and social activity: preliminary report. Available at: www.unisa.edu.au/gendered violence

McCulloch, J. and Walklate, S. (forthcoming). Rendering the ordinary extra-ordinary in order to facilitate prevention: The case of (sexual) violence against women. In C. Barlow and S. Kewley (eds) *Preventing Sexual Violence*. Bristol: Policy Press.

Merry, S.E. (2016). *The Seductions of Quantification: Measuring Human Rights, Gender Violence and Sex Trafficking*. Chicago, IL: The University of Chicago Press.

National Inquiry into Missing and Murdered Indigenous Women and Girls. (2019). Reclaiming power and place: the final report of the national inquiry into missing and murdered indigenous women and girls. Ottawa: Canada. www.mmiwg-ffada.ca/final-report/ [Accessed 5 July 2019]

Oakley, A. (2000). *Experiments in Knowing: Gender and Method in the Social Sciences.* New Press: New York.

Pierobom de Avila, T. (2018). The Criminalisation of femicide. In K. Fitz-Gibbon, S. Walklate, J. McCulloch and J.M. Maher (eds) I*ntimate Partner Violence, Risk and Security: Securing Women's Lives in a Global World*, pp. 181–198. London: Routledge.

Rafter, N. (2016). *The Crime of all Crimes: Toward a criminology of genocide.* New York: New York University Press.

Shalhoub-Kevorkian, N. (2003). Reexamining femicide: breaking the silence and crossing "scientific" borders. *Signs: Journal of Women in Culture and Society*, 28(2): 581–608.

Sherman, L. and Harris, H. (2015). Increased death rates of domestic violence victims from arresting vs. warning suspects in the Milwaukee Domestic Violence Experiment (MilDVE). *Journal of Experimental Criminology*, 11(1): 1–20.

Stockl, H., Devries, K., Rotstein, A., Abrahams, N., Campbell, J., Watts, C., et al. (2013). The global prevalence of intimate partner homicide: a systematic review. *Lancet*, 382(9895): 859–865.

Stout, K. (1992). Intimate femicide: An ecological analysis. *Journal of Sociology and Social Welfare*, 29: 29–50.

Thapar-Björkert, S., Samelius, L., and Sanghera, G.S. (2016). Exploring symbolic violence in the everyday: misrecognition, condescension, consent and complicity. *Feminist Review*, 112(1): 144–162.

True, J. (2015). Winning the battle but losing the war on violence. *International Feminist Journal of Politics*, 17(4): 554–572.

United Nations Office on Drugs and Crime. (2018). Global study on homicide: gender-related killing of women and girls. November 25 2018. Available at www.unodc.org/unodc/en/frontpage/2018/November/home-the-most-dangerous-place-for-women-with-majority-of-female-homicide-victims-worldwide-killed-by-partners-or-family--unodc-study-says.html?ref=fs1 [Accessed 29 Nov 2018]

Walby, S. and Towers, J. (2017). Measuring violence to end violence: Mainstreaming gender. *Journal of Gender-Based Violence*, 1(1): 11–31.

Walby, S., Towers, J. and Francis, B. (2015). Is violent crime increasing or decreasing? A new methodology to measure repeat attacks making visible the significance of gender and domestic relations. *British Journal of Criminology*, 56(6): 1203–1234.

Webster, K (2016) A Preventable Burden: Measuring and Addressing the Prevalence and Health Impacts of Intimate Partner Violence in Australian Women (ANROWS Compass, 07/2016), Sydney: ANROWS.

5 Using data on intimate femicide to inform risk

Introduction

So far this book has considered the ways in which counting occurs and the problems and possibilities associated with counting intimate femicide. In so doing it has considered the questions of what to count, who to count, when to count, and how we count. From these earlier chapters the risks associated with counting have become transparent. The act of counting in itself runs the risk of devaluing the lives being counted and denuding those lives of the context of their demise. Assigning a number to a death is therefore risky insofar as numbers can objectify and invisibilize the individual killed and render lives measurable when lives in fact are not like that. They can also render the perpetrator invisible. Importantly, however, it is also the case that the weight of numbers can send important messages to professionals, policy makers, and politicians in ways that individual stories may not. The risks associated with counting are nevertheless real and carry further consequences especially when the question is asked: having counted to what use is the data then put?

   The systematic gathering of quantitative data over time and in different locations can potentially indicate trends and provide valuable evidence about which policies work best to prevent intimate homicide and linked to that what theories related to violence and violence against women in particular have the most explanatory power. However, in the context of intimate femicide the already risky act of counting is rendered even more risky when the question about the use to which such data is put is asked. Much of this work has focused attention on the 'risk factors' linked with such deaths. This chapter is concerned to unpack the conundrum of using data on intimate femicides to inform risks about it and asks whether or not this knowledge can translate into meaningful change.

It should be said at the outset that despite the criminal justice embrace of risk as central to processes of prohibiting and responding to crime, 'risk' itself is a highly contested concept (Mythen 2014). Its presence and popularity in a wide range of criminal justice policies and practices, including responses to violence against women in all its forms, hides the extent to which this concept itself misunderstands and misrecognizes risk as gender neutral, culturally neutral, ethnically neutral, and disability neutral concept. Nonetheless a focus on identifying risk factors in order to prevent crime, and for the purposes of this discussion the prevention of violence(s) against women and intimate femicides, has become intimately intertwined with prevention. Thus, the central questions for this chapter are: what are seen to be the risk factors for intimate femicide, what kind of knowledge underpins these risk factors, how is risk being understood in this work, and what are the consequences of that understanding for women 'at risk' of intimate femicide? Before it is possible to consider these questions, it is useful to say something about the concept of risk itself.

Thinking about risk

Criminology, along with other social sciences, has become enamoured with the promise of risk and risk theory. This love affair has gelled well with the rise and influence of neo-liberal thinking especially within Western governments. In this context within criminal justice policy, appreciations of risk became quickly translated into the development of risk assessment tools as a means of managing the risks posed by offenders and their behaviour. However, as is the case with some romantic liaisons, the affair with risk blossomed and developed strong roots. These roots go deep and stretch out to embrace not only risky offenders but also risky victims. This 'risk creep' (Walklate and Mythen 2011) embedded risk as a forensic concept, rendering risk-based knowledge measurable and actionable, and it is a process that has particularly marked policy responses in relation to (lethal) violence against women in all its forms yet has rarely been subjected to sustained critical scrutiny.

According to Mythen (2014) there are three general limitations inherent in the social scientific embrace of risk: the limited visibility of power and power relations within risk theory, the partial view of human agency embedded within it, and the tendency towards catachresis (misapplying or overstretching the use of the concept). All of these limitations are perhaps best illustrated in the series of questions asked by Shalhoub-Kevorkian (2003: 603) as she discusses the problems associated with devising responses to femicide:

> What is the alternative if her male adult 'protector' abuses here (sexually, emotionally, physically), and how can she speak about her abuse if she has never learned that it is possible to voice personal matters? How can she speak out when she knows that customs and cultural codes may be used to cause her death? How can she ask for help when her protectors might also be her enemies? How can she trust her family when their first reactions may be to kill her? Where can she go for help when the informal agents of social control tend to blame her and question her acts? How can she ask the help of the legal system when most agents of social control are men? What happens if the legal system supports her femicide?

These questions capture beautifully the limitations embedded within the social scientific embrace of risk outlined by Mythen (2014). Power relations are rendered visible in the kinds of questions Shalhoub-Kevorkian asks, since the question of what risk itself might mean and how it might apply, if at all, in the kinds of contexts she discusses is very apt. As a consequence Shalhoub-Kevorkian also puts to the fore the question of what agency might look like under the kinds of socio-cultural conditions she describes. Put simply, what does risk feel like (especially when it is articulated as a threat to life from an intimate partner on whom you might depend) as a routine part of everyday life?

Shalhoub-Kervorkian (2003) speaks strongly to the partial understanding of risk embedded in the love affair with it found in criminal justice policy. It is a love affair that embeds a power dynamic rendering risk uniform and unifying (O'Malley 2004), actionable and measurable, and certainly in the interests of policy makers and others in the thrall of 'risk crazed governance' (Carlen 2008) rather than those on the receiving end of such policies. Thus, as this brief overview implies, risk, as a concept, is not neutral. It is structured, though the nature of that structure is frequently hidden from view. What is particularly hidden from view are the gendered assumptions underpinning it. These assumptions are prescient in the quote from Shalhoub-Kevorkian (2003) above. Nevertheless this implicit acceptance of risk as a gender-neutral concept (Walklate 1997) takes its toll on the capacity of policy to make sense of both men's and women's lives. Put simply, women are constructed as the risk-fearing, vulnerable victims with their risk-seeking behaviour hidden and/or pathologized.

Simultaneously men are assumed to be the risk seekers, thus hiding their vulnerabilities (Walklate 1997) and rendering their experiences of victimization difficult to identify, assess, and respond to. As Chan and Rigakos (2002: 756) have argued:

> [T]here can be no essential notion of risk; that risk is variable; risk itself is more than one type. ..... Women, it may be argued, are required to engage in instrumental risk in order to interact socially, work, cohabitate with a man etc. However, this does not signal women's victimhood but rather their agency in flouting potential dangers in the general pursuit of material subsistence.

In the context of living with the threat of lethal violence, women do more than 'flout potential dangers' (ibid). They negotiate, manage, and live with danger for them and their children utilizing everyday practices often rendered invisible under the veils shrouding their everyday lives framed by culture and political necessity (Shalhoub-Kervorkian 2016). Under these kinds of conditions, *what* counts as risk and *who* counts as risky is arguably quite differently informed than a gender-neutral conceptualization of risk might lead us to believe. It is possible to explore the cultural, ethnic, and disability neutral presumptions embedded in risk in very similar ways. Thus it is possible to assert who is deemed at risk, and who is deemed risky at any particular point in time, is a multi-faceted phenomenon, mediated, for example, by global geo-political positions on the one hand (Aas 2012) alongside other more local structural factors like ethnicity and culture on the other (Gill and Harrison 2016).

   In summary, whilst risk may be a useful conceptual device for policy makers (as a means for allocating scarce resources it might be argued), it offers only a partial and structurally neutral insight into the nature of the everyday world of risk in relation to lethal violence against women. Further it might be a useful tool under some conditions (discussed more fully below), but because of the theoretical limitations discussed above, its conceptual capacity to deliver on its promise is likely always to be incomplete and will always certainly be complex. However, before some of these issues are considered further, it will be useful to review what are thought to be the most common risk factors in relation to intimate femicide.

Risk factors and intimate femicide

Internationally there are two common features to homicide statistics: men are most likely to be killed by other men, and women are most likely to be killed by their (male) partner or ex-partner. For example, 79 per cent of all homicide victims globally are male and 95 per cent of perpetrators globally are also male (UNODC 2013: 13). Yet when a closer gendered look is taken at these global statistics, those most at risk from this kind of lethal violence from their partners are women aged 30 and over (see inter alia Brennan 2016 for the UK; for Europe, see Corradi and Stockl 2014; Cussen and Bryant 2015 for Australia; Smith et al. 2014 for the United States; CFOJA 2018 for Canada; and Eguizábal et al. 2016 for Latin America). Drilling down into these global figures a little further, Dobash et al. (2004), for example, reported that 76 per cent of their sample of male murderers of women had experience of relationship breakdown, with 56.9 per cent reporting previous use of violence against their partners (as compared with 60.8 per cent and 34.9 per cent respectively for the men in their sample who murdered other men). It is important to note that the maleness evidenced in these reported patterns of intimate femicide is present even in societies that enjoy relatively high levels of gender equality, such as Sweden, where intimate partner violence and gendered homicides persist. Put simply and obviously, the leading 'risk factor' for a woman to be killed is to be in or to have had an intimate relationship with a man.

The maleness of this kind of homicide has led to a consideration of whether it is particular kinds of men who are prone to this violent behaviour towards their partners. In a comprehensive overview of the research findings on whether men who kill their female partners are like other men who kill or have different characteristics, Loinaz et al. (2018) suggest that the evidence is inconclusive though there might be some mileage in looking more carefully at the factors leading to homicide more generally. This conclusion is in line with other evidence asserted by the Domestic Violence Resource Centre Victoria (DVRCV) (2016: 9), which stated that there is 'no single profile' for identifying a male offender of intimate femicide. However, there was some evidence presented by DVRCV that men who kill in this context are on average similar to the general male homicide perpetrator population, with a median age of 41 years (DVRCV 2016; see also, Bryant and Cussen 2015). In Australia, the Domestic and Family Violence Death Review Network (ADFVDRN 2018) study found that the age range for male perpetrators who killed female current or former partners during 1 July 2010 to 30 June 2014 was 19 to 82 years old, with an average age of 41 confirming the findings of the DVRCV study. In addition, there is evidence suggesting that the *motivation* for intimate femicide may be different from the motivation for homicide more generally, with sexual jealousy and beliefs in male sexual propriety featuring as the most prevalent. Indeed, Dobash and Dobash (2015: 254) found that the men in their sample constructed themselves as victims and considered their violence towards the victim as 'appropriate and justified' and 'blamed the victim in particular or women in general'. Taken together this constellation of motives is suggestive of a role for hyper-masculine values as a 'risk factor' for intimate femicide.

Researchers have gone on to identify other 'risk factors' associated with male perpetrators. In an international review of the literature on employment status as a contributory factor for intimate femicide, Kivisto (2015) reported findings ranging from 13 to 58 per cent unemployment rates among the perpetrator population. Bridger et al. (2017: 97) point to high rates of unskilled employment (at 28.9 per cent) or unemployment (at 45.5 per cent) amongst perpetrators. The DVRCV (2016) study found that just over half of the men who killed were employed at the time of the homicide, with 25 per cent unemployed. The ADFVDRN (2018) also found that almost half of the 121 male perpetrators across Australia over the 14 years of the study were unemployed at the time they used lethal violence. Campbell et al. (2003) found that rates of unemployment were higher amongst perpetrators than amongst perpetrators of (non-fatal) intimate partner violence, 49 per cent and 20 per cent respectively. Campbell et al. (2003: 1092) also concluded that 'unemployment was the most important demographic risk factor'. These differing findings support Kivisto's (2015) claims of inconsistency in rates of unemployment, pointing to a complex relationship between (un)employment and intimate femicide. Similarly varied findings are evident in relation to education. Kivisto (2015) found that half of all perpetrators had not completed a high school education. However, Dobash et al. (2009) found that men who murdered their (ex)partners were more likely to have completed a high school education than men who killed other men. Interestingly in considering risk factors pertaining to perpetrators, Bridger et al. (2017), using police data and information gleaned from domestic homicide reviews for England and Wales, suggest a key risk factor is the suicidal tendencies of the prospective offender implying a link with the risk 'toxic trio' discussed below.

In summary, there is little beyond the sex of the victim and the perpetrator to point to with confidence as a risk factor. This may be a result of, as Iratzoqui and McCutcheon (2018: 147) suggest, this area of investigation being 'largely seen as a "uniquely female" phenomena, since females are overwhelmingly the victims of this form of violence, especially over time', thus researchers have done little comparative work between different types of homicide offenders (see also Loinaz et al. 2018 cited above though; see, however, Dobash and Dobash 2015). So risky people for women seem to be men they know with hyper-masculine values and suicidal inclinations, for whom employment and education status can be a contributing factor under some conditions, though how and when is not altogether clear.

Some risk work has focused attention on the characteristics of the victim, in particular on the role of pregnancy and/or the recent birth of a child as a risk factor. While Bridger et al. (2017: 98) conclude that 'pregnancy does not seem to elevate the risk of domestic homicide', other research does suggest that pregnancy elevates at least the risk of intimate partner violence, with VicHealth (2004) suggesting 42 per cent of women who are subject to physical violence are pregnant at the time. Further research shows that family violence escalates during pregnancy and in the period immediately after childbirth (Department of Victorian Communities 2007; Taft 2002). If the escalation thesis is accepted, it follows that the risk of intimate femicide may increase during pregnancy, since the escalation thesis implies that a lethal outcome is more likely when repeated incidents of violence persist over time. This is in line with research suggesting that homicide is a leading cause of death for women during pregnancy and in the first postpartum year (see, for example, Cheng and Horon 2010; Lin and Gill 2011; Palladino et al. 2011). Digging a little deeper into these risk factors, however, the presence of mental health issues, drug use, and alcohol use (by one or both partners) are also frequently cited as constituent elements in a 'toxic trio' of risk factors (see also Gadd et al. 2019).

For example, Bridger et al.'s (2017: 97) study found that 41.1 per cent of perpetrators in their sample were substance abusers, with alcohol comprising the majority of this substance abuse (33.7 per cent). The DVRCV (2016) study uncovered similar findings, as over half of the perpetrators (*n* = 28) had a history of drug or alcohol abuse, with alcohol again being the main contributor. Kivisto (2015) further found that one in ten perpetrators had a diagnosis of substance abuse. Dobash et al. (2004), however, have argued that substance abuse is less likely in intimate femicide perpetrators, compared to men who commit other forms of homicide. The other factor forming part of this toxic trio is mental health, linking back to Bridger et al.'s (2017) observation concerning suicidal tendencies, though the role of mental health in general as a risk factor is clearly contested. Kivisto (2015) suggests that the findings of studies exploring mood disorders, such as depression, amongst perpetrators produced prevalence data ranging from 17 per cent to 56 per cent. Though as Gadd et al. (2019: 16) observe '[criminologists] must also ask why some men choose to secure control in coercive ways when so many other aspects of their lives appear out of control' as is often the case with the kinds of factors discussed above.

It is possible to disaggregate risk factors further to focus on the specific relationship dynamics most likely to result in intimate femicide. Two of note will be commented on here: risky moments and risky processes. In terms of risky moments, research work has focused attention on the presence of non-fatal strangulation in a relationship as an indicator of further violence to come. Non-fatal strangulation is known as a predictive risk factor for homicide in intimate relationships (Glass et al. 2008) and indeed features on most risk assessment tools as a result. It is certainly one of the most commonly used methods of killing in cases of this kind. For example, in an international study, Dobash et al. (2007) recorded 37 per cent of perpetrators using strangulation and the ADFVDRN (2018) attributed 15.7 per cent of the male-perpetrated deaths to strangulation and suffocation. Non-fatal strangulation is also known to have significant long-term health impacts on the victim, including cognitive changes and psychological impacts (including memory loss, fear, post-traumatic stress disorder) and physical impacts (including neck/throat pain, bruising, swelling, miscarriage, tinnitus, nausea, and so on) (Douglas and Fitzgerald 2014).

Risky processes focus attention on the process of separation. There are a number of consistent findings in the literature on this as a point in a relationship when a woman is at greatest risk (see inter alia, Dekeseredy et al. 2017; Dawson et al. 2017: 76–77). Further, Campbell et al. (2007) found that for women who have left an abusive partner, the homicide typically occurred within 12 months of the separation, indicating this remained a key risk factor for some time. Moreover, a study by the NSWDVDRT (2017) found that around one-third of the women victims in this study were killed by a former partner, and most occurred within three months of the separation (see also Campbell et al. 2003). This supports the contention that separation, or an intention or desire to separate, escalates the risk for women attempting to leave abusive relationships.

From this brief overview, it is possible to observe the kinds of risk factors that have occupied researchers engaged with understanding the characteristics and dynamics associated with intimate femicide. For ease of presentation these have been discussed in terms of their dominant focus, risky people, the constellation of risky factors, risky moments, and risky processes. Taken as a whole, this work points to some agreement on the 'risk factors' for intimate femicide. These are prior interpersonal violence, age difference (but see also the recent work of Garino et al. 2018 on the 'golden age' i.e. those over 60), co-habiting, estrangement, and the presence of a child not biologically related to the abuser. Other factors include homes where there is mental illness, drug abuse, and the presence of weapons (Campbell et al. 2007). All of this work appears to presume that the risky place for intimate femicide is the home rather than the street, though this is not often made explicit. In many ways, this work echoes the way in which risk has been embraced; as a measurable forensic concept and by implication, it erases the systemic risks deeply embedded in a wide range of geographically diverse social and cultural locations. Moreover, much of this work has been oriented towards what might be actionable on the basis of its findings. It (rather more implicitly than explicitly) endeavours to address the questions of whether, knowing the risk factors, such deaths are predictable and/or preventable. In order to move from risk factors to risk prediction/prevention, it is necessary to make certain assumptions about the way in which violence features as part of intimate partner relationships. This returns the discussion to the question of risky processes. McPhedran and Baker (2012) have made a pertinent data-led intervention on this question, which is worthy of further comment.

McPhedran and Baker (2012) suggest there are two competing perspectives in understanding the routes from non-lethal to lethal violence. The first focuses on escalation. This assumes violence escalates in a relationship over time from low risk to high risk and that there are particular turning points in this process, which can be pointed to as indicative of such escalation. The presence of non-fatal strangulation is often considered one of these points. The second focuses on the behavioural characteristics of the perpetrator. This they call a typology approach, which considers whether there are particular features of a perpetrator that may move them from a low risk of using lethal violence to high risk. They state that:

> [T]he escalation theory suggests that in the presence of 'low risk' violence, the occurrence of relationship separation is likely to predict escalation to 'high risk' violence, whereas the typology theory implies that the likelihood of lethal violence following a separation may be predicted more strongly by other behavioural characteristics previously displayed by the offender rather than by the separation event itself. Each of these scenarios suggests a different policy response, and different ways of practicing lethal violence prevention.
>
> (McPhedran and Baker 2012: 960)

They go on to point out that at present there are significant data limitations in Australia (where their work was focused) in testing either proposition effectively, particularly since the recording of non-lethal violence is especially problematic. A recent intervention by Monckton Smith (2019) based on domestic homicide review data from the UK echoes some of these observations, pointing to the different ways in which risk assessment is understood and differently informs how professionals responded to events leading up to lethal violence. Monckton Smith goes on to suggest an eight-stage model of relationships, which progressively lead to homicide based on this data. It must be noted that this model is based on data that is after the fact leaving open the question of who such a model may or may not include.

Measurement issues in this area of work are not peculiar to the Australian context. There are measurement issues relating to gendered violence at every level of data collection from the global to the local, which are compounded by measurement issues concerning what counts as violence (see, inter alia, Merry 2016). Indeed, some of these problematic issues have been discussed in the earlier chapters of this book. In effect neither the escalation nor the typology theses have been effectively tested or evidenced or such evidence that exists pertains to particular kinds of cases under particular circumstances gathered after the occurrence of the lethal violence itself. Such issues notwithstanding, there have been concerted efforts to translate the risk factors as outlined above into risk assessment instruments to inform policy and practice, and it is to those practices this chapter now turns.

Risk and Risk Assessment

Predicting fatal outcomes for intimate partner violence is fraught with difficulties, not only because of the contested nature of the risk factors as discussed above but also because less than half of intimate femicides have prior contact with the police (Thornton 2017) or any other agencies, thus rendering any link between event and intervention difficult to ascertain. However, some studies have shown that women experiencing violence are likely to provide a first disclosure to a family member or a friend, rather than a formal support service (Bagshaw et al. 2000). Bridger et al. (2017: 98) found that 'a disclosure or allegation of domestic crime had been made by the victim to a friend, family member or public agency in 60.8 per cent of cases [in their study]'. Moreover, when victims do have contact with the police, in 89 per cent of the cases Thornton (2017: 65) examined, they were not assessed as high risk – a finding endorsed by work on domestic homicide reviews (see Dawson 2017). Indeed, the relationship between having been assessed as risky and subsequent death is somewhat arbitrary

(Westmarland 2011: 300–301; see also Day et al. 2014). In fact, it is the case that many risk assessment practices assume a scalar view of violence in relationships, which may or may not exist (see inter alia Johnson et al. 2017).

Nevertheless, the use and deployment of risk assessment tools, not only for at risk offenders but also for at risk victims, has risen rapidly on policy and practice agendas. This is despite the fact that few of these tools have been subjected to empirical validation (McCulloch et al. 2016; though see Turner et al. 2019). Moreover, when they have been tested, research suggests they have a weak or modest chance at predictive power (Medina et al. 2016), can conflate prevention and prediction (O'Malley 2010), and pay little attention to the historical and social context in which such violence has occurred (Cunneen and Rowe 2015). In sum, such tools can deny the presence and influence of both structure and agency, thereby perpetuating and embedding risk as a forensically measurable and structurally neutral concept. However, not all risk assessment tools are the same so it will be of value to outline each of the main approaches in turn.

Risk assessment tools are many and varied, and there is no intention to discuss all their different properties, strengths, and weaknesses in the space provided here. Taken together, they are used to try and control the consequences of criminal behaviour. Briefly, clinical risk assessments are rooted in individual diagnostic techniques based on an historical appreciation of an individual's offending behaviour. These have a poor record of prediction and can result in both falsely predicting that behaviour will occur and it does not, and/or falsely predicting behaviour will not occur and it does. Importantly they focus on known offenders and the likelihood of them repeating their behaviour. In the context of intimate femicide, the development of the Priority Perpetrator Identification Tool (PPIT) focusing on serial domestic abusers (Robinson 2016) comes closest to constituting this kind of offender-based tool. Other risk assessment tools in the context of lethal violence against women focus more on the partner relationship and are more closely connected to actuarial risk assessment practices. These use probability statistics relating to groups of people or types of behaviour, and as a result, actuarial risk assessments are good for making predictions about groups but not so good for predicting the behaviour of individuals.

Nevertheless, contemporarily quite sophisticated risk assessment tools rooted in actuarial methods are used to assist in decision making about, and resource allocation to incidents of, intimate partner violence. These range from the spousal risk appraisal guide

(SARA), the Propensity for Abusiveness Scale (PAS), to the Partner Abuse Prognostic Scale (PAPS) (all quoted in Hoyle 2008: 327). The DASH (Domestic Abuse, Stalking and Harassment, and Honour Based Violence) model is favoured by most police forces in the UK. McCulloch et al. (2016) review a further nine tools (including DASH and SARA) designed to assess the levels of risk judged to be present for individual cases (high, medium, low). As has already been observed, and as McCulloch et al. (2016: 58) state, 'there is a paucity of empirical research evaluating the outcomes of [international] risk assessments...', and recent work suggests that the DASH tool used in England and Wales has no more predictive power than chance alone (Turner et al. 2019). Algorithmic risk assessment tools arguably take the use of probability statistics and other statistical methods to the next level. Using the techniques of machine learning, these risk assessment tools can manage a wide range of variables in complex models to inform decision making. The extent to which these kinds of tools have penetrated intimate partner violence is yet to be established.

When such tools are applied to women living with violence in all its forms, women's own knowledge of when the next act of violence is likely to occur is crucial to understanding their level of risk. Indeed Smith et al. (2010: 27) suggest this form of intimate knowledge may be deeply embedded in women's strategies for coping with 'battering', with Day et al. (2014: 581) reporting that 'approximately two thirds of victims correctly identif[ied] their assessed level of risk'. However, the extent to which women's voices are actually heard in processes of risk assessment is moot and when they are included it is frequently as a means to render them responsible for their own safety (Hoyle 2008). There are arguably a number of reasons for this, but one might be the way in which professionals in their use of such tools can also distort, resist, and draw on knowledge not reflected in the particular tool they are using in order to make a decision about a particular offender or victim (see inter alia Kemshall 2010; Robinson 2010; Werth 2017). More significantly perhaps it is possible to discern here the way in which the uncritical embrace of what risk means for whom fails to capture the reality of living in (potentially lethal) violent relationships, on the one hand, and the undoubted evidence that many women who die at the hands of their partner have never been risk assessed, on the other. Neither have their partners ever come to the attention of the criminal justice process. Inherent here are some of the dangers of relying on counting as the means by which to assess the nature and scale of intimate femicide, with risk assessment practices themselves offering only a partial insight into these issues. As Mythen (2014: 33) has commented, risk is seen as a 'master key through which the most pressing social problems of the age can be unlocked'. This discussion highlights the tangible evidence of what the embrace of risk and risk assessment pays attention to and what it does not. The presence of the bounded thinking embedded here is almost palpable (Walklate 2018). Nevertheless, risk has been an important vehicle for developing risk assessment tools that have built upon what is known about the nature of intimate femicide. However, it remains unclear what the purpose of these tools actually is.

At this juncture we are faced with a further conceptual difficulty in the deployment of risk in this way: the conflation of prevention, prediction, and protection. In many risk assessment tools, it is not clear whether their purpose is: to prevent intimate femicide, to predict when it is most likely to occur, and/or to predict a future police/service system interaction, and/or to protect the victim from further/lethal violence. The conflation of these three purposes, or at least the lack of clarity concerning them, lends weight to the view that the over-riding risk focus here is to ensure that criminal justice professionals (and others) have responded appropriately to the events presented to them rather than necessarily effectively. To this end, it is possible to suggest that in some cases the risk being mitigated is the risk to the police officer or practitioner of responding inappropriately/insufficiently, as opposed to the risk to the victim themselves.

To summarize: the unitary and unifying embrace of risk embedded in the search for risk factors and risk assessment tools reflects a partial sense of agency and stretches the concept of risk in ways in which the misrecognition of women's lives is self-evident. As a result, it is often misapplied. In relation to risk assessment tools, this embrace is as likely to result in false negatives as much as it is likely to result in false positives. Such tools also have the capacity to smooth out the peaks and troughs of people's lives presuming a linearity where none may exist (a point also made by Monckton Smith 2019) and simultaneously erase important structural differences and contexts. Thus, in failing to capture the reality of people's/women's lives, to properly count and account for the risks women face arguably amounts to risk inertia (qua Merry 2016).

Merry (2016), in discussing the processes of indicator construction at the level of the United Nations in relation to violence against women, points to the way in which various practices or inertias come to frame what is included and excluded in those indicators. Here the notion of risk inertia is intended to capture the way in which dominant understandings of risk are used, as though these understandings reflect what risk actually means for women living in situations of lethal violence when it is just as likely that they do not. Risk inertia presumes risk is measurable and individual, whereas it is also immeasurably structural and cultural (see Carrington et al. 2019: chapter 3). Indeed, as Jeffrey et al. (2018: 70) conclude, 'risk assessment, risk management, and safety planning strategies work at multiple levels', and it is important 'to consider intersecting axes of oppression and sociocultural/historical aspects of risk and experience' in individuals' whole circumstances. This is a particularly pertinent observation in relation to Indigenous women but not exclusively so. There is, however, another issue here. Again following Merry (2016) this might be called time inertia.

The concept of time inertia carries with it two implications. The first refers to how concepts and/or policies become 'locked in' over and through time. The discussion above offers some insight into the ways in which risk has become 'locked in' to discourses around lethal violence. In a similar vein, Walklate and Hopkins (2019) have discussed the ways in which policy responses to gender-based violence have also become 'locked in' over and through time. The second implication of foregrounding time inertia refers back in the first instance to the 'escalation thesis', as articulated by McPhedran and Baker (2012) discussed above. Much work in the prevention field operates from the presumption that violence in relationships escalates over time. This presumption pays scant regard to those relationships in which violence might have featured but has come to an end and/or those relationships in which the first act of violence might in fact be the lethal one. Much could be learned from both contexts in relation to developing a thick approach to prevention. As was discussed earlier, currently available data does not permit the effective testing of this escalation thesis and/or the lacunae it contains. In addition the presumption of linearity over and through time embedded in the popular embrace of the escalation also demands closer scrutiny. The presumption of linearity is also part of time inertia. If these two features are taken side by side, it is possible to envisage the ways in which temporality is smoothed out and even erased from measurement, risk, prediction, prevention, and protection. Referring back to the earlier discussion in this book of slow femicide, the case there was made for appreciating the loss of 'life' for women whose lives are permeated with stress, anxiety, ill-health, and early death as a result of living with violence. These experiences can and do permeate lives above and beyond their own and can travel through families across the generations. The measurement focus of risk, compounded by risk inertia, is further compounded by the incident-led, linear focus flowing from time inertia, framing the policy imaginations generated by both of them. All of this happens in the absence of evidence that captures the complexities of women's (and men's) lives living with violence as 'just part of life' (Genn 1988).

Conclusion

The linear, uniform, and unimaginative embrace of risk and time has fuelled a wide range of work concerned to itemize separate and separable risk factors contributing to intimate femicide. This has also provided the knowledge base on which risk assessment practices have grown apace, with some of those practices travelling from one context to another as though differences in history and culture do not matter. The incremental way in which risk has penetrated policies and practices designed to respond to lethal violence against women clearly takes a particular toll on those for whom risk carries different meanings, particularly those of different culture, ethnicity, or ability (Cunneen and Rowe 2015) and for whom challenging the everyday violence(s) in their lives can be insurmountable (Shalhoub-Kevorkian 2016). The structural inclusionary and exclusionary practices of counting lethal violence through the lens of risk, risk factors, and risk assessment also reflect the danger of assuming that such lethal violence is the preserve of those younger, able-bodied men and women whose lives are characterized by the 'toxic trio'. This would be a mistake, as some of the evidence cited in this chapter demonstrates. At the same time, some of these same women living with these 'risks' are able to get on with their lives and move beyond the violence endemic within them. These women stand as testimony not only to the prevalence of risk inertia but also to the resistances to it. They also serve to remind us of the importance of understanding *processes* as articulated over and through time – processes in which people can and do change. Listening to their voices might afford a route out of the blinkered vision of risk and time reflected in much of the work cited here. These voices also afford a salutary listening post for those who might over-invest in the virtues of counting. At the same time, the review offered in this chapter also illustrates the individualized assumptions embedded in the embrace of risk and time and where this leads in relation to prevention. As the work of the CFOJA (2018) led by Myrna Dawson illustrates, the complex interplay between individual, communal, societal, cultural, and historical factors that can result in intimate femicides not counted and not acted upon. This poses some important questions for the relationship between counting and prevention, explored more fully in the next chapter.

References

Aas, K.F. (2012). 'The earth is but one but the world is not': criminological theory and its geopolitical divisions. *Theoretical Criminology*, 16(1): 5–20.

Australian Domestic and Family Violence Death Review Network (ADFVDRN). (2018). Data report 2018, Sydney.

Bagshaw, D., Chung, D., Couch, M., Lilburn, S., and Wadham, B. (2000). Reshaping responses to domestic violence, final Report. Australia: University of South Australia.

Brennan, D. (2016). *Femicide Census Profiles of Women Killed by Men: Redefining an Isolated Incident*. London: Women's Aid.

Bridger, E., Strang, H., Parkinson, J., and Sherman, L.W. (2017). Intimate partner homicide in England and Wales 2011–2013: pathways to prediction from multi-agency domestic homicide reviews. *Cambridge Journal of Evidence Based Policy*, 1: 93–104.

Bryant, W. and Cussen, T. (2015), Homicide in Australia 2010–11 to 2011–12: national homicide monitoring program report, Australian Institute of Criminology Monitoring Report no. 23, Canberra.

Campbell, J.C., Glass, N., Sharps, P.W., Laughon, K., and Bloom, T. (2007). Intimate partner homicide: review and implications of research and policy. *Trauma, Violence & Abuse*, 8(3): 246–269.

Campbell, J.C., Webster, D., Koziol-McLain, J., Block, C., Campbell, D., Curry, M.A., and Laughon, K. (2003). Risk factors for femicide in abusive relationships: Results from a Multisite Case Control study. *American Journal of Public Health*, 93: 1089–1097.

Canadian Femicide Observatory for Justice and Accountability (CFOJA). (2018). 106 women and girls killed by violence: eight month report. Available at: https://femicideincanada.ca/sites/default/files/2018-09/CFOJA%20FINAL%20REPORT%20ENG%20V3.pdf

Carlen, P. (2008). Imaginary penalities and risk crazed governance. In P. Carlen (ed) *Imaginary Penalities*, pp. 1–25. Cullompton, Devon: Willan.

Carrington, K. Hogg, R., Scott, J., Sozzo, M., and Walters, R. (2019) *Southern Criminology*. London: Routledge.

Chan, W. and Rikagos, G. (2002). Risk, crime and gender. *British Journal of Criminology*, 42(4): 743–761. doi: 10.1093/bjc/42.4.743

Cheng, D. and Horon, I.L. (2010). Intimate-partner homicide among pregnant and postpartum women. *Obstetrics & Gynaecology*, 115(6): 1181–1186.

Corradi, C. and Stöckl, H. (2014). Intimate partner homicide in 10 European countries: Statistical data and policy development in a cross-national perspective. *European Journal of Criminology*, 11(5): 601–618.

Cunneen, C. and Rowe, S. (2015) Decolonising indigenous victimisation. In D. Wilson and S. Ross (eds) *Crime, Victims and Policy: International Contexts, Local Experiences*, pp. 10–32. London: Palgrave-MacMillan.

Cussen, T. and Bryant, W. (2015). Domestic/family homicide in Australia, Australian Institute of Criminology Research in Practice no. 38, Canberra.

Dawson, M. (ed) (2017). *Domestic Homicide Reviews: An International Perspective*. London: MacMillan-Palgrave.

Dawson, M., Jaffe, P., Campbell, M., Lucas, W., and Kerr, K. (2017). Canada. In M. Dawson (eds) *Domestic Homicide Reviews: An International Perspective*. London: MacMillan-Palgrave.

Day, A., Richardson, T., Bowen, E., and Bernardi, J. (2014). Intimate partner violence in prisoners: toward effective assessment and intervention *Aggression and Violent Behavior*, 19: 579–583.

DeKeseredy, W.S., Dragiewicz, M., and Schwartz, M.D. (2017). *Abusive Endings: Separation and Divorce Violence against Women*. Oakland: University of California Press.

Department for Victorian Communities. (2007). Family violence risk assessment and risk management: supporting an integrated family violence service system, Family Violence Coordination Unit, Melbourne.

Dobash, R.E. and Dobash, R.P. (2015). *When Men Murder Women*. New York: Oxford University Press.

Dobash, R.E., Dobash, R.P., and Cavanagh, K. (2009). 'Out of the blue': men who murder an intimate partner. *Feminist Criminology*, 4(3): 194–225.

Dobash, R.E., Dobash, R.P., Cavanagh, K., and Lewis, R. (2004). Not an ordinary killer – just an ordinary guy: when men murder an intimate woman partner. *Violence Against Women*, 10(6): 577–605.

Dobash, R., Dobash, R., Cavanagh, K., and Medina-Ariza, J. (2007). Lethal and non-lethal violence against an intimate female partner. *Violence against Women*, 13(4): 329–353.

Domestic Violence Resource Centre Victoria ('DVRCV'). (2016). Out of character? Legal responses to intimate partner homicides by men in Victoria 2005–2014, Discussion Paper No. 10.

Douglas, H. and Fitzgerald, R. (2014). Strangulation, domestic violence and the legal response. *Sydney Law Review*, 36(2): 231–254.

Eguizábal, C., Ingram, M., Curtis, K.M., Korthuis, A., Olson, E.L., and Phillips, N. (2015). Crime and violence in Central America's Northern Triangle: how U.S. policy responses are helping, hurting, and can be improved. Washington, District of Columbia: Wilson Center.

Merry, S.E. (2016). *The Seductions of Quantification*. Chicago, IL: University of Chicago Press.

Gadd, D., Henderson, J., Radcliffe, P., Stephens-Lewis, D., Johnson, A., and Gilchrist, G. (2019). The dynamics of domestic abuse and drug and alcohol dependency. *British Journal of Criminology*, advance access, azz011, doi:10.1093/bjc/azz011

Genn, H. (1988). Multiple victimisation. In M. Maguire and J. Ponting (eds) *Victims of Crime: A New Deal?*, pp. 88–98. Buckingham: Open University Press.

Gerino, E., Caldarera, A., Curti, L., Brustia, P., and Rollè, L. (2018). Intimate partner violence in the golden age: systematic review of risk and protective factors. *Frontiers in Psychology*, 9 article 1956.

Gill, A.K. and Harrison, K. (2016). Police responses to intimate partner sexual violence in South Asian communities. *Policing*, 10(4): 446–455.

Glass, N., Laughon, K., Campbell, J., Chair, A., Block, C., Hanson, G., Sharps, P., and Taliaferro, E. (2008). Non-fatal strangulation is an important risk factor for homicide of women. *Journal of Emergency Medicine*, 35(3): 329–335.

Hoyle, C. (2008). Will she be safe? A critical analysis of risk assessment in domestic violence cases. *Children and Youth Services Review*, 30(3): 323–337.

Iratzoqui, A. and McCutcheon, J. (2018). The influence of domestic violence in homicide cases. *Homicide Studies*, 22(2): 145–160.

Jeffrey, N., Fairbairn, J., Campbell, M., Dawson, M., Jaffe, P., and Straatman, A-L. (2018). Canadian Domestic Homicide Prevention Initiative with Vulnerable Populations (CDHPIVP) Literature Review on Risk Assessment, Risk Management and Safety Planning. London, ON: Canadian Domestic Homicide Prevention Initiative.

Johnson, H., Eriksson, L., Mazarolle, P., and Wortley, R. (2017). Intimate partner femicide: the role of coercive control. *Feminist Criminology* online first. doi:10.1177/1557085117701574

Kemshall, H. (2010). Risk rationalities in contemporary social work policy and practice. *British Journal of Social Work*, 40(4): 1247–1262.

Kivisto, A.J. (2015). Male perpetrators of intimate partner homicide: a review and proposed typology. *The Journal of the American Academy of Psychiatry and the Law*, 42(3): 300–312.

Loinaza, I., Marzabalb, I., and Andrés-Pueyoa, A. (2018). Risk factors of female intimate partner and non-intimate partner homicides. *The European Journal of Psychology Applied to Legal Context*, 10(2): 49–55.

Lin, P. and Gill, J.R. (2011). Homicides of Pregnant Women. *American Journal of Forensic Medical Pathology*, 32: 161–163.

McCulloch, J., Maher, J.M., Fitz-Gibbon, K., Segrave, M., and Roffee, J. (2016). Review of the Family Violence Risk Assessment and Management Framework (CRAF): Final Report. Melbourne, Australia: Monash University.

McPhedran, S. and Baker, J. (2012). Lethal and non-lethal violence against women in Australia: measurement challenges, conceptual frameworks, and limitations in knowledge. *Violence Against Women*, 18(8): 958–972.

Medina, A.J., Robinson, A., and Myhill, A. (2016). Cheaper, faster, better: expectations and achievements in police risk assessment of domestic abuse. *Policing*. Epub ahead of print 2 July 2016. doi: 10.1093/police/paw023

Monckton Smith, J. (2019). Intimate partner femicide: using Foucauldian analysis to track an eight stage progression to homicide. *Violence Against Women*. doi.org/10.1177/1077801219863876

Mythen, G. (2014). *Understanding the Risk Society*. London: Palgrave.

New South Wales Domestic Violence Death Review Team ('NSWDVDRT'). (2017). Report 2015–2017, Sydney.

O'Malley, P. (2004). *Risk and Uncertainty*. London: Glasshouse Press.

O'Malley, P. (2010). *Crime and Risk*. London: Sage.

Palladino, C.L., Singh, V., Campbell, J., Flynn, H., and Gold, K.J. (2011). Homicide and suicide during the perinatal period. *Obstetrics & Gynaecology*, 118(5): 1056–1063.

Robinson, A. (2016). Serial domestic abuse in wales: an exploratory study into its definition, prevalence, correlates, and management. *Victims & Offenders*. doi:10.1080/15564886.2016.1187691

Shalhoub-Kevorkian, N. (2003). Re-examining femicide: breaking the silence and crossing 'scientific' borders. *Signs*, 28(2): 581–608. doi: 10.1086/342590.

Shalhoub-Kevorkian, N. (2016). The occupation of the senses: the prosthetic and aesthetic of state terror. *British Journal of Criminology*. Advance access 10 September 2016. doi: 10.1093/bjc/azw066

Smith, S.G., Fowler, K.A., and Niolon, P.H. (2014). Intimate partner homicide and corollary victims in 16 states: National Violent Death Reporting System, 2003–2009. *American Journal of Public Health*, 104(3): 461–466.

Smith, P.H., Murray, C.E., and Coker, A.L. (2010). The coping window: a contextual understanding of the methods women use to cope with battering. *Violence and Victims*, 25(1): 18–28.

Taft, A. (2002). Violence against women in pregnancy and childbirth: current knowledge and issues in health care responses, Issues Paper 6, Australian Domestic and Family Violence Clearinghouse, University of New South Wales.

Thornton, S. (2017). Police attempts to predict domestic murder and serious assaults: is early warning possible yet? *Cambridge Journal of Evidence Based Policing*, 1: 64–80.

Turner, E., Medina, J., and Brown, G. (2019). Dashing hopes? the predictive accuracy of domestic abuse risk assessment by police. *British Journal of Criminology*, advance access, azy074, doi:10.1093/bjc/azy074

UNODC. (2013). *Global Study on Homicide 2013.*

VicHealth. (2004). The health costs of violence: measuring the burden of disease caused by intimate partner violence, Victorian Health Promotion Foundation, Carlton.

Walklate, S. (1997). Risk and criminal victimisation: a modernist dilemma? *British Journal of Criminology*, 37(1): 35–45.

Walklate, S. (2018). Criminology, gender and risk: the dilemmas of northern theorising for southern responses to intimate partner violence. *International Journal for Crime, Justice and Social Democracy*, 7(1): 4–16.

Walklate, S. and Hopkins, A. (2019). Real lives and lost lives: making sense of 'locked in' responses to intimate partner homicide. *Asian Journal of Criminology*, 14: 129–143. doi:10.1007/s11417-019-09283-2

Walklate, S. and Mythen, G. (2011). Beyond risk theory: experiential knowledge and 'knowing otherwise.' *Criminology and Criminal Justice*, 11(2): 99–113.

Werth, R. (2017). Individualizing risk: moral judgement, professional knowledge and affect in parole evaluations. *British Journal of Criminology*, 57(4): 808–827.

Westmarland, N. (2011). Co-ordinating responses to domestic violence. In J. Brown and S. Walklate (eds) *Handbook of Sexual Violence*, pp. 287–307. London: Routledge-Willan.

Conclusion
Looking to the future – from counting to preventing?

Introduction

The United Nations has called on every nation to engage in counting femicides and to do so by setting up femicide watches. The world today is more focused on violence against women than it ever has been. The call for the greater attention to counting femicides is in line with the push to collect better data on violence against women in all its forms. The rationale behind the push to more systematically quantify, measure, and count violence against women is multifaceted. Such counts are aimed at making violence against women more visible and harnessing that visibility and the weight of numbers produced towards the ultimate goal of ending violence against women. The counting of these killings is generally understood as aimed at protecting lives.

The femicide counts that currently take place around the world have typically been instigated by feminist scholars, journalists, advocates, and activists in the face of the deficiencies and violence(s) of institutionalized data. These counts have been motivated in some instances by the desire of women to acknowledge the violent and untimely deaths of other women; to confront the social structures that deny, minimize, and normalize such deaths; and to take action to change the circumstances and silences that support the types of behaviours and attitudes that lead to such killings. Ultimately it is hoped that better counting will lead to better accountability for such deaths at all levels of society: individual, community, and at the social and structural levels. In this book we have focused on the problems and possibilities that potentially attach to the more systematic counting of intimate femicides. Intimate partner violence is the most common type of violence against women worldwide, and intimate femicide is the most extreme expression of intimate partner violence. Violence against women remains at epidemic proportions and is globally endemic.

Ending violence against women is undoubtedly a long-term goal. It will certainly take more than a generation. From where we are today it may seem impossible. However, as Max Weber (1946: 28) observed, 'historical experience confirms the truth – that man [*sic*] would not have attained the possible unless time and time again he [*sic*] reached out for the impossible'. While gender inequality remains ubiquitous in many countries and has been sustained over many generations, the actions of women in one generation have transformed the lives of future generations of women. In her book *If Women Counted*, which is about the failure of the national accounts to count women's domestic labour, Marilyn Waring (1988: 326) wrote:

> We women are visible and valuable to each other, and we must, now in our billions, proclaim that visibility and that worth. Our anger must be creatively directed for change. We must remember that true freedom is a world without fear. And if there is still confusion about who will achieve that, then we must each of us walk to a clear pool of water. Look at the water. It has value. Now look into the water. The woman we see there counts for something. She can help to change the world.

Waring's book focused on the need to count women's labour outside the formal workforce as real labour. In the second edition of the book, written more than ten years on, she reflects on her earlier work and in particular her advocacy for the centrality of counting as a strategy to make women's work count. Here she comments on the limited ability to capture women's lived experience through the medium of counts and the resilience of the system, while purporting to count women's labour, to completely misunderstand, minimize, and deny the value of that labour. In short, Waring concludes as we have been careful to argue throughout this book, being counted is not the same as counting. Counting is a tool. It reinforces and reflects a series of empirical and ideological commitments about what counts as knowledge. It can be a powerful tool, both as a weapon of oppression and as a means of resisting oppression. However, it can also reinforce existing invisibilities and often does so particularly for marginalized and minoritized peoples.

Counts of intimate femicide alone are ultimately unlikely to be unable to bring into focus the broader social structures and ongoing histories of colonialism that support such lethal violence. Counts alone will also likely fail to bring into view the untimely deaths of women who have endured intimate partner violence. A woman may survive an act or acts of violence at the hands of her violent intimate partner or partners. The aftermath of such violence, however, including significant economic and health impacts, may end her life earlier than would have otherwise been the case. The link between intimate violence and untimely death is deeply embedded in the social, economic, cultural, and political structures that devalue women's lives and fail to adequately protect, support, and restore women and their children from the immediate and ongoing, sometimes intergenerational, harms that arise from intimate violence. Excavating these links is a matter of seeing and knowing, an act of imagination in a world where the power/knowledge dyad is, if not inescapable, at least deeply imbricated in all our lives. Women's lives are not just taken by their violent partners but they are narrowed and disappeared by embedded social structures so pervasive that we fail to see them. Capturing the violence beyond the individual intimate femicide cannot be done numerically. So we must be cautious, explicit, and alert: counting alone is not going to create change. Data alone cannot move us towards prevention. As the quote from Waring above suggests, the real source of transformative power is not found in counting but in the social movement of people concerned to achieve social change. Preventing femicide must include dismantling the social hierarchies that create fertile ground for the killing of women by their male partners and make it so difficult for so many women to find or regain safety and security in their everyday lives.

Counted or counting?

There is a long history of women as property and men as property owners. Wives and daughters have historically and continuously, in many ways and in many places, been treated as the chattels of the male head of the family and ruler of the home. Intimate femicide is often a reflection of male proprietary privilege. Women are at higher risk of being killed by their male intimate partner at the time of separation, and this is a clue to the salience of such control: classically expressed as 'if I can't have you then no one can'. The violent trope of 'killing my woman' goes beyond just the expression of sexual jealousy and the protection of male honour, a common emotion amongst men. It is linked to men's sense of entitlement to retain control and dominion over a woman, who is reduced in the eye of the perpetrator to an object, existing only as an extension of self.

Violence against women is mundane, ordinary, and an everyday occurrence: 'Just part of life' (Genn 1988: 98). Violence against women is ordinary and 'folded into everyday life' (Das 2007: 14). If violence is an everyday occurrence, then we have to ask what dangers lie in capturing only the extremes, such as intimate femicides, as a marker of violence against women. Does it illuminate the whole, the continuity of everyday violence(s), or does the extreme occlude the continuity from the everyday? There is a danger that we can lose texture and complexity by simply focusing on being counted as opposed to actually counting. Counting in a meaningful way implicates all of techniques, processes, and gaps of the count. It asks that the act of counting ensures those responsible for intimate femicide are also persistently and consistently called to account. Put simply, it is important to ensure counts focus as much if not more on the offenders, whilst simultaneously affording memory justice to the victims. Alternatively, what results are counts that fail to count. Otherwise, as Merry (2016: 219) states, 'measurement makes this visible while the measured disappear'. So, why count?

Why count (reprised)?

If the dangers of counting as outlined in this book and intimated in the paragraph above are both manifest and manifold, why count? We hope that in these pages we have developed a convincing enough argument to suggest that counting can be an important means to an end. The weight of numbers affords the opportunity of different layers of influence from the global to the local. It is self-evident that the costs of such deaths, however they are counted, matter to national economies, to the global economies, and to the capacity for half the world's population to contribute meaningfully to the societies in which they can live free from fear, threat, and injury from those who proclaim to love or care for them. The consequences of not counting deny the contribution of those lives to the well-being of all even when there might be issues of indigeneity, disability, ethnicity, culture, and belief interfering with an appreciation of their contribution.

So counting matters to ensure women's lives lost to men's lethal violence count. At the same time, practices of counting need to be sensitive to the complexities of real lives that may result in such violence. As the Canadian Femicide Observatory for Justice and Accountability (CFOJA, 2019) report has observed, there is no single factor that can predict femicide; neither is there one simple prevention strategy. The risks are complex and layered. So prevention strategies and how we think about prevention itself also need to be complex and layered. If this awareness is built into how we count and what counting is used for both imaginatively and practically, then it may be possible to reap some rewards from the numbers, hold those responsible to account, and ensure women's lives across the globe lost to lethal violence have counted. Such a commitment has implications not only for how such lives are measured but also how sense is made of the statistics gathered and what is done on the basis of them. Such a commitment recognizes the explicitly political work of remembering and memorializing each woman killed at the hands of a male intimate or as a result of male violence that is found in installations and art works such as 'Il Muro Di Bambole' ('The Wall of Dolls'), the red shoes in Mexico (Telesur 2016), or red dresses in Canada blowing in the wind, remembering the First Nations women killed (Coorsh 2015). These are an important part of how we count, remember, and acknowledge what is still unseen and uncounted.

Counting to preventing: looking to the future?

To quote Merry (2016: 222) again, 'We rely on numbers alone at our peril', and indeed it has been the intention of this book to elaborate some of those perils. Moreover in her account of the ways in which indicators of all kinds are produced in seeking the possibility of universal counts, Merry (2016) makes clear that this search for commensurability requires whatever it is being measured is removed from its embeddedness. Of course what results from these processes of removal are measures that create homogeneity where none may exist. There are geo-political contexts in which femicide occurs, or has occurred, with impunity (the Northern Triangle in Latin America for example), and there are others where the tensions between the colonizers and the colonized are contributory to the patterns of femicide documented (as in Canada for example), as we have documented in the pages of this book. We have been keen, despite the 'seductions' (Merry 2016), to encourage a healthy scepticism of the extent to which commensurability on its own can offer a guide to the nature and extent of femicide in the contemporary (complex) global world. In this spirit we have added the phenomena of risk inertia and time inertia to Merry's concepts of data inertia and expertise inertia. It is also possible that the phenomenon of spatial inertia makes its presence felt in the processes of data construction, with which we have been concerned here in which the hegemonic practices of the global north subsume the realities of life in the global south (see Connell 2007). We are, however, in agreement with Merry insofar as we are aware that '[t]he indicators and the knowledge they create reinforce the theory they embody' (Merry 2016: 208). This observation sits alongside the call by Walby and Towers (2017) for a better conceptual base from which to make sense of the statistics on violence against women that takes account of their gendered nature. However, it also seeks to develop that conceptual thinking a little further and moves us on to consider the question of prevention.

McCulloch and Walklate (forthcoming) identify six models of prevention. These include the mechanistic (a simple cause-and-effect model); the ecological model (the one favoured by the World Health Organisation and the one most deeply embedded in much of the work in this field); the spectrum of prevention model (a development of the ecological model); the responsive model (which focuses on what violence means for all the participants and how to respond on that basis); and the whole family model (the newcomer to the field and prioritizes working with all the family members concerned not solely with the victim and perpetrator). As has been stated, the ecological model has been favoured globally and has become increasingly embedded in work in this field. This model assumes there is no one single cause of violence (against women or otherwise) but rather that violence is the outcome of how different factors relating to the individual, their relationships, the community, and society interact with one another. The value of this model, in terms of prevention, is that it turns the professional gaze away from a search for individual pathology in either the victim or the perpetrator and directs attention to wider structural, cultural, and historical inequalities, which when overlaid on one another contribute to the complex web of human lives and their capacities for dealing with the challenges posed by that complexity. However, there are limits to this ecological gaze. These limits emanate from its inherent functionalist view of societies and social processes. As a result, in practise, it embeds a limited view of power, power relations, and the capacity of individuals to negotiate these. In other words, it also embeds a limited view of human agency. It is no great surprise, therefore, that it melds well with the policy embrace of risk in which, as discussed in Chapter 5, an understanding of power and agency are also limited. Thus the ecological model assumes that some individuals and/or groups are at greater risk of interpersonal violence than others and other individuals and/or groups are more protected from it. This assumption leads to interventions for prevention, primary, secondary, and tertiary, that rest on evidence associated with such risk factors and how these risk factors have been understood. Yet, as we have argued, risk is at least gendered, raced, ableist, and necessarily partial, incomplete, confused, and complex. It is perhaps no great surprise that as a result the preventive strategies embodying such an understanding of risk result in interventions reliant on what might be called 'thin' counts – that is, counts which both circumscribe and minimize the prevention gaze.

More recent iterations of this counting →intervention→ prevention vision have become more complex, seeking to build a more dynamic, interactive, and integrated account of how the different features of violence in people's lives work differently in different contexts (see, for example, Heise 2011). The theme of integration is pursued in Cohen and Swift's (1999) model of a spectrum of prevention, which is in effect a more nuanced understanding of the ecological model. This model assumes the need for comprehensive and collaborative initiatives at each level of the ecological model. The spectrum of prevention focuses attention on strengthening individual knowledge and skills at the level of the professional, to promoting community education, educating providers, fostering coalitions and networks, changing organizational practices, and influencing policy and legislation (Cohen and Swift 1999: 203–207). This approach centres the cause of violence squarely in the realm of the social and embraces collaboration as a key feature of prevention. All the elements of this approach demand effective information sharing systems and processes. Indeed, whatever model of prevention that flows from the implicit acceptance of the ecological model of violence, they all rely on collaboration and information sharing across a wide range of agencies. However, if any intervention strategies emanating from the ecological model are to 'work', it is necessary to think through the role of violence in people's real lives as opposed to how they might be imagined by policy makers. This is especially the case when those real lives might be differently informed about the nature of roles and responsibilities in different communities, cultures, and countries when those lives are not necessarily characterized by the kind of functionalist view of society implicit in the ecological mode or prevention. In particular, visions of intervention, including the ecological model, need to embrace the thorny issue of the problematic behaviour of men and the power relations that support, 'turning a blind eye to', and/or endorse that behaviour in the interests of sustaining gendered power relations. Otherwise what results is 'thin' intervention: a logical outcome of 'thin' counts. It is at this juncture that it might be worth reflecting on, and creating a space for, what might be called 'thick intervention' stemming from 'thick counts'.

Thick counts, which are arguably the kinds of counts we have been proposing in this book, not just focus attention on numbers and risk factors but situate each of these within structure, culture, time, and space. Thus numbers and risk factors become overlaid not only with the lives lost as a result of violence even if not fatally (slow femicide) and the lives lost as a result of lethal violence (intimate femicide) but also with the processes of calling perpetrators, policy makers, and politicians to account. This would constitute thick counting providing the basis for thick intervention. Put simply, the way in which gender is ordered can be both the cause and the excuse for both individual and collective behaviour. Tackling femicide demands ongoing vigilance at all of these levels in order to resist co-option and to ensure appropriate prioritization in theory, policy, and practice. In this sense, the personal is still very much political. In order to ensure 'thick' intervention, following Ackerly and True (2018), it is important to render a critical gendered lens normative, so that patterns of gender oppression, privilege, and entitlement are not hidden or obscured but are rather illuminated and exposed. In the face of 'backlash', in all its different forms it requires centring patriarchy in our theory and practice of counting (Dekeseredy 2019). If we are to make our counts of women who have been killed count, we need to be accountable first and foremost to them, the lives they have lived, and what we have lost collectively in their untimely deaths. It is only when we commit to 'thick counts' and the 'thick prevention' that follows that we may see some inroads into what in the twenty-first century seems to be an intractable global problem of intimate femicide.

Postscript: towards a global femicide index?

There have been a number of starting points to the concerns addressed in this book shared between us as authors. One of them has been to encourage some critical thinking within the academy and policy about what security means and who constitutes the security threat (Walklate et al. 2017). In the course of this conceptual excavation, we were made acutely aware of the disconnect between the funds spent on 'big security' driven by the increasing global concern with the threat from terrorism and the paucity of funding in comparison spent on 'little security', the everyday threats faced by women from men (see Fitz-Gibbon et al. 2018). This disconnect is even more remarkable in those societies in which the threat from terrorism is a small risk when considered against the funds spent on the terrorist threat when compared with violence against women (see Walklate et al. 2017). At the same time the interconnections between these two agendas have been for the most part silenced within the academy and policy (notable exceptions are Smith 2019; McCulloch et al. 2019). As the recognition that the 'homegrown' terrorist is also the man who is violent to women and to other men grows, it is also important to note that this interconnect matters everywhere. If the findings of the UNODC (2018) on the nature and extent of violence against women, including intimate femicide, were

put alongside the Global Terrorism Index (2018), a remarkably similar symmetrical pattern would emerge. In other words, whilst there
are different peaks and troughs recorded in each of these indices over
time, the gendered ordering of the findings they each contain remains
the same. As Connell (2016: 15) has observed:

> a cultivated callousness is involved in organizing abduction of
> girls, suicide bombings, femicide, beheadings, and mass addition.
> It seems close to the callousness involved in drove strikes, mass
> sackings, structural adjustment programmes, nuclear armaments,
> and the relentless destruction of our common environment.

Here Connell is centring the gender order as the lens through which to
appreciate these interconnections. Similarly, a global femicide index,
constructed sensitively and acutely aware of the politics inherent in
counting and what such counts might mean to whom, needs also to
be aware of its own political role. Consequently, there is an important space for such indices to act as an integrated knowledge base on
femicide: to offer both a point of counting, a centre from which to
generate meaningful and culturally sensitive practices of prevention,
and a place in which those lives lost to intimate femicide may be af-
forded memory justice. In other words, such indices cloud add to the
disconnections commented on above and elsewhere in this book, or
they could challenge them. We would prefer the latter.

References

Ackerly, B. and True, J. (2018). With or without feminism? Researching gender and politics in the 21st century. *European Journal of Politics and Gender*,
1(1–2): 259–278.

Canadian Femicide Observatory for Justice and Accountability (CFOJA).
(2019). #CallitFemicide: understanding gender related killings of women and
girls in Canada 2018. Available at: www.femicideincanada.ca (Accessed 5
June 2019).

Connell, R. (2007). The northern theory of globalisation. *Sociological Theory*,
25(4): 368–385.

Connell, R. (2016). 100 million Kalashnikovs: gendered power on a world
scale. *Feminista*, 51: 3–17.

Cohen, I. and Swift, S. (1999). The spectrum of prevention: developing a comprehensive approach to injury prevention. *Injury Prevention*, 5: 203–207.
Available at: www.preventioninstitute.org

Coorsh, K. (2015). Red dresses honour Canada's missing and murdered Aboriginal Women. *CTV News*. October 4 2015. Available at: www.ctvnews.

ca/canada/red-dresses-honour-canada-s-missing-murdered-aboriginal-women-1.2594856

Das, V. (2007). *Life and Words; Violence and the Descent into the Ordinary.* Berkeley: University of California Press.

Dekeseredy, W. (2019). Bringing feminist sociological analysis of patriarchy back to the forefront of the study of woman abuse. Paper presented to the 3rd European Conference on Domestic Violence, Oslo, September.

Fitz-Gibbon, K., Walklate, S., McCulloch, J., and Maher, J. (2018). *Intimate Partner Violence, Risk and Security: Securing Women's Lives in a Global World.* London: Routledge.

Genn, H. (1988). Multiple victimisation. In M. Maguire and J. Pointing (eds) *Crime Victims; A New Deal?* pp. 88–98. Milton Keynes: Open University Press.

Heise, L. (2011). What works to prevent partner violence: an evidence overview. London: Strive.

Institute for Economics & Peace. Global Terrorism Index. (2018). Measuring the impact of terrorism, Sydney, November 2018. Available at: http://vision ofhumanity.org/reports (Accessed 28 July 2019)

McCulloch, J. and Walklate, S. (forthcoming) Rendering the ordinary extraordinary in order to facilitate prevention: The case of (sexual) violence against women. In C. Barlow and S. Kewley (eds) *Preventing Sexual Violence.* Bristol: Policy Press.

McCulloch, J., Walklate, S., Maher, J., Fitz-Gibbon, K., and McGowan, J. (2019). Lone Wolf Terrorism through a gendered lens: men turning violent or violent men behaving violently? *Critical Criminology: An International Journal.* doi:10.1007/s10612-019-09457-5

Merry, S.E (2016). *The Seductions of Quantification: Measuring Human Rights, Gender Violence and Sex Trafficking.* Chicago, IL: The University of Chicago Press.

Smith, J. (2019). *Home Grown: How Domestic Violence Turns Men into Terrorists.* London: Riverun.

Telesur. (2016). Mexico: impunity high as femicide memorial remembers victims, 15 March 2016. Available at: www.telesurenglish.net/news/Mexico-Impunity-High-as-Femicide-Memorial-Remembers-Victims-20160315-0020.html

United Nations Office on Drugs and Crime (UNODC). (2018). Global study on homicide: gender-related killing of women and girls. United Nations Office on Drugs and Crime, Vienna. Available at: www.unodc.org/documents/data-and-analysis/GSH2018/GSH18_Gender-related_killing_of_women_and_girls.pdf (Accessed 14 June 2019)

Walby, S. and Towers, J. (2017). Measuring violence to end violence: mainstreaming gender. *Journal of Gender-Based Violence*, 1: 11–31.

Walklate, S., McCulloch, J., Fitz-Gibbon, K., and Maher, J.M. (2017). Criminology, gender and security in the Australian context: making women's lives matter. *Theoretical Criminology.* doi:10.1177/1362480617719449

Waring, M. (1988). *If Women Counted: A New Feminist Economics.* Toronto: University of Toronto Press.

Waring, M. (1999). *Counting for Nothing: What Men Value and Women Are Worth*. Toronto: University of Toronto Press.

Weber, M. (1946). Politics as a vocation. In H. Gerth and C.W. Mills (eds) *From Max Weber: Essays in Sociology*, pp. 77–128. New York: Oxford University Press.

Webster, K. (2016). A preventable burden: measuring and addressing the prevalence and health impacts of intimate partner violence in Australian women (ANROWS Compass, 07/2016), Sydney: ANROWS.

Index

Ackerly, B. 65, 72
ADB *see* Asian Development
  Bank (ADB)
ADFVDRN *see* Australian Domestic
  and Family Violence Death Review
  Network (ADFVDRN)
Africa 34–6
alcohol abuse 81, 83
Anderson, R. 27
Asia 1, 34, 36
Asian Development Bank
  (ADB) 38
Australia 1, 8, 22, 50, 52–3, 80
Australian Domestic and Family
  Violence Death Review Network
  (ADFVDRN) 24, 79, 80
Australian Institute of Criminology 22

Baker, J. 83, 88
Barnes, R. 7
Barnwell, A. 12
Bayatrizi, Z. 50, 66, 67
'Black Lives Matter' movement 52
Booth, J.W. 26
Bradshaw, R. 60
Bridger, E. 80, 81, 84

Caman, S. 67
Campbell, J.C. 80
Canada 27, 38–9, 63, 71
Canadian Femicide
  Observatory for Justice and
  Accountability (CFOJA) 10, 21–2,
  35, 54, 89, 97
Caribbean 39

CFOJA *see* Canadian Femicide
  Observatory for Justice and
  Accountability (CFOJA)
Chan, W. 78
Cohen, I. 100
Connell, R. 102
Corradi, C. 63, 66, 68
'Counting Dead Women' in Australia
  10, 25, 26
counting, femicide 3–6, 48–50, 96–8;
  advocacy 25–6; costs of 11–13;
  data gaps 62–4; deaths 52–3;
  domestic homicide death reviews
  23–4; epistemological framework
  64–8; femicide observatories 21–3;
  international 20–1; monitoring
  programmes 21–3; practices of
  64–8; prevention of 98–101; risks
  of 60–72; value of 60; violence
  53–6; visual memorialization 26–8
crime statistics 54, 55
Cullen, P. 48
'cunning of history' 7

DASH *see* Domestic Abuse, Stalking
  and Harassment, and Honour
  Based Violence (DASH)
data gap 62–5
Dawson, M. 23, 61, 89
Day, A. 86
deaths 52–3; cross national borders
  52; family homicide death reviews
  23–4; intimate partner violence 35;
  male intimate partner in Africa 36;
  violent civilian deaths 52

Dekeseredy, W. 7
'Destroy the Joint' movement 25
Dobash, R.E. 13, 22, 79, 80, 82
Dobash, R.P. 13, 22, 79, 80
Domestic Abuse, Stalking and
  Harassment, and Honour Based
  Violence (DASH) 86
domestic homicide death reviews 23–4
Domestic Violence Resource Centre
  Victoria (DVRCV) 79, 80
Donovan, L. 7
dowry-related deaths 33, 36–7
DVRCV *see* Domestic Violence
  Resource Centre Victoria (DVRCV)

ecological model 61, 99
economic costs 11
El Salvador 1, 36
England 1, 10, 80, 86
EOF *see* European Observatory of
  Femicide (EOF)
epistemological framework 64–8
European Observatory of Femicide
  (EOF) 22

family homicide death reviews 23–4
family violence 1, 23, 24, 37, 69–70
femicide; *see also* intimate femicide:
  counts (*see* counting, femicide);
  economic costs of 11; global
  issue 9–11; Latin America
  39–40; monitoring programmes
  21–3; observatories 2, 19, 21–3;
  prevalence of 10; risks, counting of
  60–72; watches 2, 19, 21–3
'Femicide Census' in England 10,
  25, 26
Foucault, M. 49
Fraser, N. 7

Gadd, D. 81
Gender Equality Observatory for
  Latin America and the Caribbean
  (GEO) 22
gender-neutral concept 77, 78
gender-related killing 6, 11, 20, 62, 67
gender violence 5, 9, 68, 71, 84
GEO *see* Gender Equality
  Observatory for Latin America
  and the Caribbean (GEO)
Global Homicide Report 62

global intimate femicide rate 33–4
Global Terrorism Index 102
Grosz, Elizabeth 4

heterosexual intimate partner
  homicide 8
Hirsch, M. 28
homicide 3, 79; data 84; domestic
  death reviews 23–4; statistics 8, 55,
  78; suicides 55
The Homicide Report, New
  Zealand 35
Honduras 36, 55
honour killings 33, 37, 38
Hopkins, A. 88
human rights 46, 49–51

If Women Counted (Waring) 3, 95
ILO *see* International Labor
  Organisation (ILO)
India 37
indigenous women and girls, killing
  27, 33, 38–9, 41
international counts 20–1
International Labor Organisation
  (ILO) 4
International Tribunal on Crimes
  against Women 6
interpersonal violence 82–3, 99
intimate femicide 8, 20; *see also*
  femicide; counting 46–56; global
  death rates 33–4; global issue
  9–11; motivation 79; national
  death rates 34–6; prevention of
  61; recognizing of 70; risk of
  40–1, 75–89; unrecorded 36–9;
  unreported 36–9
intimate partner violence (IPV) 2,
  6–9, 46–9, 64
IPV *see* intimate partner
  violence (IPV)
Iratzoqui, A. 80

Jeffrey, N. 88

Kivisto, A.J. 80

LAFO *see* Latin American Femicide
  Observatory (LAFO)
Lale-Demoz, A. 21
Latin America, law reform 39–40

Latin American Femicide
  Observatory (LAFO) 22
lethal violence 83–4, 89
Loinaza, I. 79

McCulloch, J. 86, 99
McCutcheon, J. 80
McPhedran, S. 83, 88
Manjoo, Rashida 37
memorialization *see* visual
  memorialization
memory justice 26
Merry, S.E. 13, 49, 64, 68–70,
  87–8, 98
Mexico 1, 25, 27, 35, 98
Monckton Smith, J. 84
monitoring programmes 21–3
Mythen, G. 76, 77, 86

national femicide monitoring
  programmes 21–3
National Homicide Monitoring
  Program (NHMP) 22, 24
National Inquiry into Missing and
  Murdered Indigenous Women and
  Girls, Canada 28, 38
national intimate femicide rates 34–6
New South Wales Domestic
  Violence Death Review Team
  (NSWDVDRT) 82
New Zealand 35, 41
NHMP *see* National
  Homicide Monitoring
  Program (NHMP)
Nixon, R. 11
non-fatal strangulation 82
non-lethal violence 83–4
Norman, D. 60
NSWDVDRT *see* New South Wales
  Domestic Violence Death Review
  Team (NSWDVDRT)

Oakley, A. 64
Olive, P. 11

PAPS *see* Partner Abuse Prognostic
  Scale (PAPS)
Partner Abuse Prognostic Scale
  (PAPS) 86
PAS *see* Propensity for Abusiveness
  Scale (PAS)

Pickering, S. 52–3
Pillay, N. 37
PPIT *see* Priority Perpetrator
  Identification Tool (PPIT)
pregnancy, risk of 81
prevalence: gendered violence
  71; honour killings 37;
  intimate partner violence 9;
  violence 20
Priority Perpetrator Identification
  Tool (PPIT) 85
Project DAPHNE 35
Propensity for Abusiveness Scale
  (PAS) 86

Radford, J. 12
Rafter, Nicole 69
Red Heart Campaign 26–7
'red shoes' movement 27
responsive model 99
results-based policy development
  69–70
Rigakos, G. 78
risk 76–8; assessment 84–9;
  counting 40–1; data gaps 62–4;
  epistemological framework 64–8;
  and intimate femicide 78–84;
  practices of counting 64–8;
  structural violence 69–70
risk crazed governance 77
Russell, D. 6, 12
Rwandan genocide 69

SDA *see* Sustainable Development
  Agenda (SDA)
separation, process of 82
sexual and gender-based violence
  (SGBV) 63
sexual violence 40, 69, 80–1
SGBV *see* sexual and gender-based
  violence (SGBV)
Shalhoub-Kevorkian, N. 62, 63, 66,
  72, 77
Sheehy, E.A. 7
slow femicide 12
Smith, K.I. 25, 26, 35
Smith, P.H. 86
Smith, V. 28
social movements 50
social science research methods 64
South-East Asia 20, 37

spectrum of prevention model 99, 100
spousal risk appraisal guide 85
Stockl, H. 7
Stout, K. 63
structural violences 69–70
suicides 8, 37, 55
Sustainable Development Agenda
    (SDA) 5
Swift, S. 100
symbolic violence 61, 71

terrorism 10–11
Thapar-Björkert, S. 61
The National Inquiry into Missing
    and Murdered Indigenous Women
    and Girls, Canada 71
The Seductions of Quantification
    (Merry) 49
thick counts 100–1
thick intervention 100–1
thin counts 99, 100
thin intervention 100
Thornton, S. 84
time inertia 88
Towers, J. 5, 7, 54–6, 62, 65, 98
True, J. 63, 65, 68, 72, 101

unemployment 80
United Nations Office on Drugs and
    Crime (UNODC) 11, 20–1, 34–8,
    101; Global Study 40
United States 8–10, 23–5, 27, 34

UNODC *see* United Nations
    Office on Drugs and Crime
    (UNODC)
unreported and unrecorded intimate
    femicides 36–9

Vatnar, S.K.B. 55
VicHealth 81
violences 9; data 6; deaths 52; forms of
    10; gender (*see* gendered violence);
    prevalence of 20; structural
    (*see* structural violences); women
    and intimate femicides 53–6
visual memorialization 26–8

Walby, S. 5, 7, 11, 13, 54–6, 62, 65,
    67, 68, 70, 98
Wales 1, 10, 80, 86
Walklate, S. 88, 99
Waring, M. 3–4, 95
Weber, L. 52–3
Weber, M. 95
*What Is to Be Done about Violence
    against Women?* (Wilson) 5
Wilcox, D. 26
Wilson, E. 5
'Women Count USA' 26
Women's Aid 25, 35
women's domestic labour 3–4
Wonders, N. 11
World Health Organisation (WHO)
    20, 46

For Product Safety Concerns and Information please contact our EU
representative GPSR@taylorandfrancis.com
Taylor & Francis Verlag GmbH, Kaufingerstraße 24, 80331 München, Germany

www.ingramcontent.com/pod-product-compliance
Ingram Content Group UK Ltd.
Pitfield, Milton Keynes, MK11 3LW, UK
UKHW021421080625
459435UK00011B/109